Emergency Management for Healthcare, Volume V

Emergency Management for Healthcare, Volume V

Writing an Emergency Plan

Norm Ferrier

BEP
BUSINESS EXPERT PRESS
Leader in applied, concise business books

Emergency Management for Healthcare, Volume V:
Writing an Emergency Plan

Copyright © Business Expert Press, LLC, 2023.

Cover design by Charlene Kronstedt

Interior design by Exeter Premedia Services Private Ltd., Chennai, India

First published in 2022 by
Business Expert Press, LLC
222 East 46th Street, New York, NY 10017
www.businessexpertpress.com

ISBN-13: 978-1-63742-411-7 (paperback)
ISBN-13: 978-1-63742-412-4 (e-book)

Business Expert Press Healthcare Management Collection

First edition: 2022

10 9 8 7 6 5 4 3 2 1

This book is dedicated to my loving wife and most stalwart supporter—
Jennifer Johnson.

Description

This series of books focuses on highly specialized Emergency Management arrangements for healthcare facilities and organizations. It is designed to assist any healthcare executive with a body of knowledge which permits a transition into the application of Emergency Management planning and procedures for healthcare facilities and organizations.

This series is intended for experienced practitioners of both healthcare management and Emergency Management and also for students of these two disciplines.

Keywords

emergency; disaster; mass-casualty event; healthcare; hospital; specialty facility; triage; Disaster Plan; Mass Casualty Plan; Evacuation Plan; staff training; university program; critical incident; Command-and-Control; Incident Management System; disaster recovery

Contents

Acknowledgments

No body of knowledge is ever singular, and no book is ever written in isolation. The author wishes to thank the following individuals—friends certainly, but also both colleagues and mentors, for their reviews and critiquing of material and for their support and guidance in this project:

Eric Dykes, PhD, Professor of Emergency Planning and Disaster Management (retd.), University of Hertfordshire, Hatfield, UK, and Past President, Institute of Civil Protection and Emergency Management, UK.

Gerald Goldberg, PhD, Professor of Psychology, York University, Toronto, Canada.

Daniel Klenow, PhD, Professor of Emergency Management, University of North Dakota, USA.

Margaret Verbeek, CEM, Past President, International Association of Emergency Managers.

How to Use This Series

This series of books is intended to provide the student of EM with a comprehensive introduction to the practice of this discipline within the specialized context of a healthcare setting. It deals with the practice of EM from the "ground up," introducing all of the basic concepts and skills, but in the context of healthcare settings. Healthcare institutions, such as hospitals and specialty care facilities, by the very nature of their business, operate with variables which are not normally found in the community at large, and therefore, require more attention than normally occurs in community Emergency Plans. All of the expected subjects will be covered in some degree of detail. Each chapter will focus on a different aspect of EM, always within the specialized context. That is not to say that the content would not be applicable in other types of EM in fact, the opposite is quite true.

Each chapter contains both theory and practical applications. In terms of chapter organization, in each case the applicable theory will be addressed, followed by examples which are, wherever possible, specific to the healthcare setting. The examples are then followed by the identification of location-specific problems and by the development of appropriate strategies to address and resolve each type of problem identified. Following each chapter's conclusion, a series of student projects are recommended, each with the intent of developing the student's experience at the application of practical skills. These are followed by a series of multiple-choice questions, intended to provide the student with a knowledge check prior to moving on to the next chapter. Finally, a list of recommended readings, along with citations, and end notes for the content of each chapter are included. The author recognizes the fact that we live in an increasingly digital world and that good textbooks are becoming increasingly expensive and difficult for both students and their learning institutions to acquire. As a result, wherever possible, instructions have been provided in each citation for accessing the appropriate reference information source online. Additionally, wherever possible, the recommended reading list includes instructions to access the entire books digitally.

This series of books is not just intended for a student audience. Working Emergency Managers in both healthcare settings and in community and government settings will hopefully find this information useful and practical. As a result, the author has attempted to include actual examples of the majority of the document types described in the various chapters of this book. These are available digitally, on a copy-protected website, access to which accompanies this book at the time of sale. The website is formatted to permit the viewing of the documents, but not the printing of those documents, and without the ability to modify the documents in any way. As a major labor-saving device, the reader may purchase a password-protected one-year renewable license, which will unlock the content of the website, permitting the full customization of each document to reflect local realities, including specific site locations, local telephone numbers, and even the logo of the reader's institution. In essence, this feature permits the rapid development of a comprehensive Emergency Response Plan, and all of the associated documentation, for any type of hospital or other healthcare institution. Information on obtaining such a license is included on the inside leaf of this book.

Introduction

This series of books is intended to teach the skills which have been traditionally associated with the practice of Emergency Management (EM). This includes all of the skills involved in the assessment of risk, selection of Command and Control models, the writing of an Emergency Plan, the testing of that document by means of various types of exercises, and the development of employee education programs which are intended to strengthen familiarity with the plan. However, no Emergency Plan is a "blueprint" to guide a community or organization through its successful response to a disaster. Every disaster is different in multiple ways and is extremely complex. If we could simply preplan and preprogram every type of emergency response from start to finish successfully, we would be in possession of crystal balls, and the need for Emergency Managers would be minimal.

This series of books differs from other well-written and useful Emergency Management textbooks in two important respects. First, it will deal exclusively with the practice of Emergency Management as it should occur specifically within a healthcare setting. Second, it will attempt to introduce the use of contemporary mainstream business planning practices to the practice of Emergency Management, something with the potential to build bridges between the Emergency Manager and the senior executive who has little knowledge or understanding of the subject.

The application of Emergency Management to a healthcare setting is essential. It can be argued that any healthcare institution is, in fact, a highly specialized community. It can also be argued that virtually every type of service or agency found in a normal community has some type of counterpart within the specialized community of a healthcare setting. It is also important to remember that the vast majority of a community's most vulnerable population will typically be found within some sort of healthcare setting, whether an acute care hospital, a specialty care hospital, or a long-term care facility. In order to mitigate against such vulnerabilities and to protect those who possess them, a certain degree of understanding of the clinical context is required. The clinical context is, in the majority of cases, a substantive source of each individual's vulnerability. This is not to say that the Emergency Manager must be an expert clinician, but they do need to possess an understanding of relevant clinical issues. In Emergency Management, the best Emergency Manager available cannot simply be "dropped" into a hospital to work, any more than they can do so in an oil refinery, a postsecondary institution, a busy international airport, or any other highly specialized institution.

This series of books will attempt to introduce several new mainstream business and academic concepts into the practice of Emergency Management. These will include formal Project Management, applied research methodology, root cause analysis, Lean for Healthcare, and Six Sigma. All of these concepts have a potentially valuable contribution to make to the effective practice of Emergency Management. Of equal importance is the fact that for many years the Emergency Manager has been challenged to affect the types of preparedness and mitigation-driven changes that are required within the organization or the community. Part of this has been the challenge of limited resources and competing priorities, but an equally important aspect of this has been the fact that the Emergency Manager has typically used a skill set and information generation and planning processes which were not truly understood by those to whom they reported and from whom they required project approval.

These mainstream business and academic processes and techniques are precisely the same ones which are used to train senior executives and CEOs for their own positions. As a result, the information generated is less likely to be misunderstood or minimized in its importance, because it comes from a process which the senior executive knows and uses every working day. This "de-mystifies" the practice and the process of Emergency Management, giving the Emergency Manager, and Emergency Management itself, dramatically increased understanding and credibility, potentially making the Emergency Manager a "key player" and contributor to the management team of any organization in which they work, and far more likely to be regarded as an expertise resource.

CHAPTER 1

Writing an Emergency Plan

Introduction

The Emergency Plan is central to the process of Emergency Management; without one, the Emergency Manager is left to react to each crisis as it occurs, often with poor results. I would explain why it is important to have a plan (beyond stating "poor results") and the value of the planning process. Historically, Emergency Plans have been generic in nature, using what has been described as an "all-hazards" approach, with a generic response process and a generic set of response tools, which were modified to meet the needs of whatever adverse event happened to occur. Generally, the "all-hazards" plan is a base plan, which is typically supplemented by hazard or incident-specific plans. In this respect, the healthcare setting has been somewhat more advanced with respect to Emergency Plans, with case-specific planning occurring for several decades now. This chapter will describe the process of writing an Emergency Plan, along with describing the most essential elements of a good plan.

This chapter will focus on the creation of the Emergency Plan for a healthcare setting, using the tools of Project Management,[1] Lean,[2] and Six Sigma[3] wherever possible. The various approaches to plan creation will be discussed, along with specific procedures for creation of an effective Emergency Response Plan for use in a healthcare setting. The type of plan model being proposed is innovative and is intended to describe a "best practice" for the creation of Emergency Response Plans for a healthcare setting, one which is easy to follow and use and which satisfies all of the legal requirements, as well as the requirements of the accreditation process. It will incorporate the information already covered in Chapters 1 to 6, in order to help the student to create the most effective plan possible.

Learning Objectives

At the conclusion of this chapter, the student should be able to describe the various approaches to the creation of an Emergency Plan, describing the advantages and the disadvantages to each approach. The student should be able to describe the process of creating an Emergency Plan as a formal project and understand how to apply the Project Management process to the creation of the plan. The student should be able to describe the process for creating an Emergency Plan, including all the essential elements of a plan for a healthcare setting. The student should understand how mainstream business processes, such as Project Management, Lean, and Six Sigma, can be applied to the creation of an Emergency Plan, in order to make the document more effective. The *how* is the easy technical part—more important for students to understand the *why* and the purpose it serves.

What Is an Emergency Plan?

Emergency Plans will vary from organization to organization, and each is created, based upon the specific needs of the organization which created it and also upon the knowledge and skill of the author. The term "Emergency Plan" is somewhat generic. In the United States, such documents are often referred to as "Emergency Operations Plans," while in still other jurisdictions, the term "Disaster Plan" is still in use. There are, however, some commonalities which should be explored. An Emergency Plan is *not* a step-by-step blueprint, intended to guide the reader through the entire emergency; this is a popular misconception. A well-written Emergency Plan is a roadmap of sorts, intended to guide the reader quickly and efficiently through the activation and the deactivation of the organization's emergency response apparatus whenever adverse events preclude the use of normal, day-to-day plans. While some commonalities do exist, all emergencies, and their responses, are different; they deal, in large measure, with the initiation and the standdown of the response mechanisms and resources; after the first hour, your will still have to "fly by the seat of your pants." But staff will have established the response processes correctly, and now success or failure will be dependent upon the resources which are available and upon the judgment and decision-making skills of those responding to the emergency.

An Emergency Plan is a guide to the activation and deactivation of the emergency response process.[4] An effective plan recognizes the fact that, in most healthcare facilities, key decision makers are not in the building 24 hours per day, and so, must provide approved and effective guidance to more junior staff, in order to function in those circumstances which cannot await the arrival of the more Senior Management Team. It is intended to provide clear instructions to staff who may have never encountered an (routine emergencies, minor, significant or major) emergency or had need to use the plan before, so that response is not delayed until senior decision makers can arrive.

An additional part of its function is to identify compliance with the legal and other official (e.g., accreditation) standards which have been placed upon the organization. The purpose of preparing the plan is not to meet accreditation, but rather to guide the organization through what the expected response is to an emergency. Having said that, the Joint Commission or like accreditation organizations will expect the healthcare facility to have an Emergency Plan and a program—and a plan is *not* an Emergency Management program. It identifies authority to act, procedures for activation and deactivation, spending authority, and accountability. Concept of operations—what is the plan? What is the strategy? What are the planning assumptions? What are we trying to achieve? What are the planning goals and objectives? How are we going to assemble as a team—in person or virtually—to make what strategic decisions? What strategic decisions should we be thinking about in advance of an emergency? What are our emergency procedures, and what kind of things do we need to have protocols/policies/procedures for? What are the expectations of the board? And the people we serve? It clearly explains the process that the organization intends to use in order to respond to the emergency, including the Command and Control system to be used, Key Roles and general emergency responsibilities, key emergency-specific facilities, and specific instructions for staff regarding specific issues (e.g., dealing with the media). As such, it is an essential method of demonstrating that the healthcare organization which created it has demonstrated "due diligence" in dealing with the response to emergencies. More importantly, executive leaders want to make sure that we have a plan in place should a disaster occur and want to be sure it is practical and that key staff are trained and know what to do.

Each organization has its own specific reasons for the creation of an Emergency Plan. While local, regional, and national laws generally operate in the case of communities, hospitals and other healthcare facilities are only sometimes specifically mentioned in legislation or regulations, and those regulations which apply to public hospitals may not necessarily apply to privately operated hospitals which receive no public funding. Indeed, many hospitals around the world are more likely to be compliant with the standards provided and monitored by one or more of the several international accreditation bodies which operate in healthcare. These bodies *do* understand the importance of effective emergency planning in healthcare facilities. It is regarded as an essential component of their periodic accreditation and is considered to constitute both good governance and due diligence! Plans were in place before they were mandated. Anybody that understands a bit about risks realizes you need a plan for your risks and hazards. Hospitals may or may not have a legal mandate for the creation of a plan; this is a matter for the pertinent legislation of the local jurisdiction. They do, however, generally regard the presence of an Emergency Plan as a best practice, and again, depending upon the organization, as an accreditation standard.

Long-term care facilities and other types of healthcare organizations may or may not be subject to regulations generated by pertinent governing legislation, but almost all are also subject to accreditation of some type. It is interesting to note that the accreditation issue, along with the fact that most healthcare agencies deal with emergencies on some scale on an almost daily basis (routine emergencies), has resulted in a far greater level of interest in the subject in healthcare, than in municipalities, which sometimes, unfortunately, simply regard their requirement for an Emergency Plan as "yet another unfunded mandate." Why not make the case that institutions should factor in the cost of emergency preparedness no different than how they budget for equipment and for supplies. CEOs want a resilient organization and having a solid Emergency Plan is one aspect of resiliency.

The Emergency Plan as a Project

Like many of the advance aspects of Emergency Management, the creation of the Emergency Response Plan is, in fact, a project consisting of a series of smaller projects. As such, it is amenable to the principles and techniques of Project Management and, as previously demonstrated, with the creation of the Hazard Identification and Risk Assessment (HIRA).[5] One of the major objectives should be, wherever possible, to create a plan which standardizes the work of responding to each type of emergency—a key principle of Six Sigma.[6] If work is standardized, potential errors in performance can be reduced or eliminated, and it becomes possible to monitor individual performance for compliance; staff are more likely to use the Emergency Plan in the manner originally intended.

This is the time to look at the proposed response measures and methods critically. If the Emergency Manager is about to develop standardized work models, using checklists, for example, the plan creation process is the correct time to actually analyze the proposed measures critically. Analysis should occur even to the point of using the Value Stream Mapping techniques.[7] Doing so is likely to identify weaknesses in current procedures and to identify and eliminate wasted time and resources. As a result, the opportunity is provided to potentially make many emergency response processes simpler and more efficient. The resulting processes are likely to be easier for staff to understand and remember and, therefore, less subject to error—once again, an opportunity to put the principles of Six Sigma in operation.

This is also an appropriate time to utilize applied research skills. Before implementing a technique or a process, take the time to ensure that the technique or process is the best one available. To illustrate, if the Emergency Manager is about to incorporate a mass-casualty triage process into the Emergency Plan, it is prudent to conduct a literature search on the subject, in order to identify whether a new model of triage which might better meet the needs of the organization is available. Similarly, polling or surveying other facilities, in the local region or elsewhere, might also identify specific information, which is useful, but was previously unknown. This can be a somewhat complex project, and certainly time-consuming for the Emergency Manager; however, time

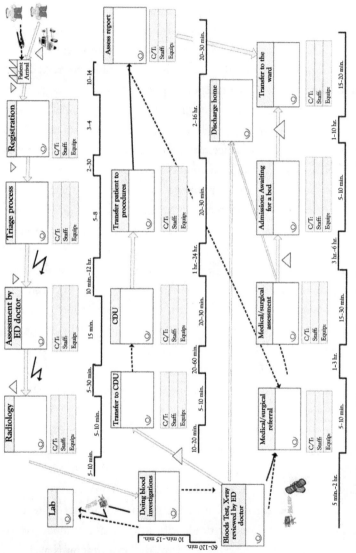

Figure 1.1 Value Stream Mapping can be applied to any process, including emergency treatment and throughput, to improve both efficiency and overall performance

spent now by the Emergency Manager and others has the potential to greatly reduce or even eliminate time wasted by others, during any future crisis. Once again, this is a key principle of Lean for Healthcare.[8]

The creation of an Emergency Response Plan is also an opportunity for teamwork, collaboration, and consensus building, by the Emergency Manager. By creating an Emergency Preparedness Committee for the purpose of creating the plan, a number of critical objectives can be achieved. By selecting committee members from a broad range of the organization's work areas, the Emergency Manager creates a pool of expertise about the organization, its strengths and weaknesses, and how it functions.[9] By encouraging participation in the creation process by others, a sense of "ownership" and "buy-in" of processes and procedures, and even of the plan itself, begins to develop. The new plan begins to acquire a collection of "ambassadors" or even "champions" to the balance of the organization. Of course, in such a huge project, the significance of the old saying that "many hands make light work" should not be lost on the Emergency Manager! Even when some members of the group are not actually writing policies or procedures for the plan, they constitute a significant representative "sounding board" for those policies and procedures and will remain useful long after the Emergency Plan is completed. Build ownership among stakeholders.

The degree of complexity and of work required will be determined in large measure by the current state of the organization's Emergency Response Plan. There are several variables which must be considered. If a plan exists, it may be possible to simply review and update the existing document, with appropriate updating of policies and procedures. This will largely be dependent on whether or not, in the opinion of the Emergency Manager, the existing plan could actually be operationalized during an emergency; an Emergency Plan which cannot be operationalized is essentially useless to the organization. Consider the potential usefulness of an "Emergency Plan" describing the use of resources or personnel which simply do not exist in the facility, and the impact of trying to rely on such a plan during an actual emergency event. Revision of the existing plan will also be determined to some extent on the plan format which was used by the previous author; is it in a format which is in current use, and will it lend itself to ease of usage for the staff? Risks are by no means

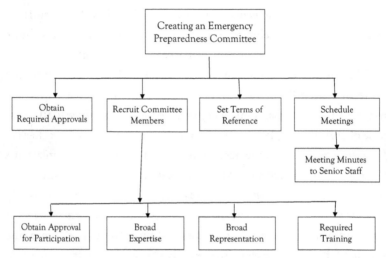

Figure 1.2 The emergency prepared committee: Essential to the creation of an effective emergency preparedness program

static; issues such as facility operations, risks, and exposures to them are in a state of perpetual evolution, just like the facility itself. The facility probably bears only passing resemblance to what it looked and worked like 10 years ago; then why wouldn't the development and pattern of both risks and risk exposure evolve continually, along with the facility itself? The process of conducting a formal HIRA process is annual and the plan needs to be updated and reviewed annually and following actual incidents, as you "build back better."

The final factor which must be considered is the age of the existing plan. A plan which is more than two years old is considered to be out of date, in many jurisdictions. If an organization changes its structure and/ or the responsibilities, the plan needs to change and adapt to what is new. Age is not the only factor. A plan can be out of date because legislation changed. Recent events and exposures, such as COVID-19, can also profoundly affect the currency of an emergency, with lessons learned from the event necessitating an immediate and complete revision of the plan. Any plan which is more than five years old is likely to be so far out of date in terms of both content and format that it is easier for the Emergency Manager to start again from the beginning.

For the purposes of this chapter, a project for the creation of a brand-new Emergency Response Plan for a healthcare institution will be described. The project is described in a linear manner, and the process of creation may be accelerated somewhat through the use of concurrent steps, if the Emergency Manager has the resources to do so. But building and maintaining a current Emergency Response Plan is an iterative process and the plan is a "living document."

Essential Elements

In the past, most Emergency Plan documents were binders written in a narrative format and often very difficult in which to find appropriate information quickly. In many cases, within the healthcare setting, the tendency was to introduce the document to new staff during new employee orientation, but with little or no follow-on training. The difficulty of use of the document meant that the staff very rarely read any portion of the

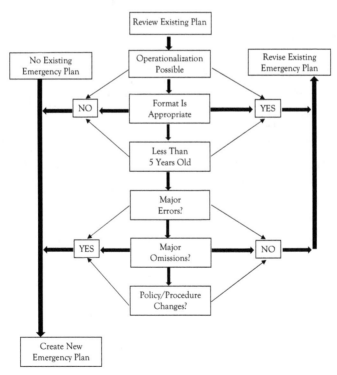

Figure 1.3 A logical project plan for determining whether to revise or replace an existing Emergency Plan

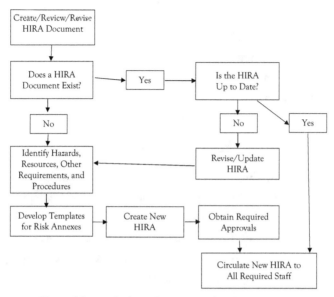

Figure 1.4 Formal hazard identification and risk assessment conducted during the planning process ensures that the plan remains relevant

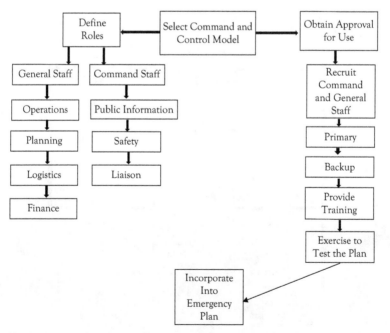

Figure 1.5 Choosing an effective and consistent Command and Control model increases plan effectiveness

document on their own, unless an emergency occurred. During an emergency, the binder would often be pulled out to consult, but after difficulties were encountered in finding appropriate information, it would frequently be tossed to one side, and the staff would begin doing what they thought was best (freelancing). This was hardly surprising, since, in many cases, most members of the management team had never read the document either! There was a standing joke that the Emergency Plan provided valuable service as a doorstop in the CEO's office, to be pulled out and dusted off a few months before accreditation was due. The value is in the process, so no one has to pull out the plan because they have learned it and should now have a one-page Job Action Sheet for all essential positions.

All good contemporary Emergency Plans will contain certain key elements, each of which has its own purpose to serve. The staff should not have to waste large amounts of time searching for information, instead of doing productive work; this is an essential principle of Lean for Healthcare. Staff time is too valuable and important to be wasted! Each additional minute that a staff member has to spend searching for information is a minute that they are not spending on bringing the emergency event to a resolution, and the impact can "balloon"! To illustrate, if the incident is currently escalating, it will continue to escalate further every minute that remedies are not being applied. If the staff member is busy hunting for difficult-to-access instructions and deciding whether they have the authority to act or whether these instructions apply in this specific circumstance, the event will continue to escalate, and its results will continue to worsen, until the actual attempt to resolve the event begins.

The result is not only a waste of staff time, but also a potentially unnecessary amount of damage, disruption of service, economic loss, and, in healthcare, even the loss of lives. An Emergency Plan is supposed to assist and provide guidance to staff responding to an emergency, not to disrupt and delay that response! An appropriately written plan is divided into clear and distinct elements, in order to provide ease of access to specific types of information. These include the main body of the plan, annexes, appendixes, and Job Action Sheets. The plan is only a guideline and is only good until the ball gets hiked. That is why practice is important, because what you planned for may not be the real-life scenario, but many of the impacts you may face are the same across so many different types of emergencies. Patients may have to be evacuated for a number of reasons, but you have to have a strategy for multiple situations—slow onset (move most critical first) versus sudden with no warning (ambulatory first) horizontal, vertical, out of the building, and so on.

Main Body

The main body of any Emergency Plan is the part which, to the reader, looks most like a traditionally written plan. It deals with those issues which are universally applicable. These include authority to activate, incident command system, and spending authority. The style is primarily narrative and covers all of the legal elements required in such a document. Key elements include a title page, record of amendments,[10] and a table of contents. It also includes a statement of authority, which identifies who specifically authorized the creation of this plan and may also make reference to specific legislation[11] or industry standards, such as accreditation standards,[12] which mandated the creation of the document.[13] A statement of scope should also be included.[14] This element identifies precisely, for the reader, what the plan document is intended to address and achieve and also what it is not intended to address and achieve.

The main part of the plan is the concept of operations: what is our strategy? How are we going to handle this crisis? What measures are we going to put into place, who is going to do what, what are the authoritative instructions that we need to issue? and so on. How do we communication internally, externally, and by what means—emergency mass notification system? In addition to identifying a Command and Control model such as the Healthcare Incident Command System (HICS)[15] or the Healthcare Emergency Command and Control System (HECCS),[16] this section of the plan will also outline communications procedures.

This section of the plan will also identify the location, structure, and function of certain emergency-specific resources, such as the Hospital Command Center, family information center, media information center, and staff staging area, which will be determined by the nature of the emergency and the requirements of the facility to manage it. This section of the plan will also specify reporting requirements, including reporting to senior staff of the organization, the community itself, and senior levels of government. Finally, it will provide a clear statement of the authority to stand down and instructions on how this is to be accomplished, once the emergency event has concluded.

Which clinical specialties exist in what other hospitals, if there are even any nearby? If the facility must evacuate, who goes where? Which staff will accompany patients during evacuation transport? What is the procedure for various types of evacuations? Who has the authority to order any of these measures and under what circumstances? How will the healthcare facility interact with the municipal Emergency Operations Center? Does our plan rely realistically on local Emergency Medical Service for evacuation, or do alternate arrangements need to be in place in advance?

When composed according to the ease of access principles of Lean for Healthcare, the document should have not only a table of contents, but also numbered pages. Wherever possible, the format of the document should be "one issue per page" with any overflow being placed on the back surface of each page. A glossary of terms should also be included, in order to ensure that the reader has a precise understanding of the intended meaning of each key word or phrase, to eliminate any potential misunderstanding arising from misinterpretation.[17]

In addition to making information much easier for the reader to find, the manual may be designed so that staff using it may be able to literally pull out the relative page, using it as an instruction sheet, which greatly increases compliance with the content of the plan. Moreover, this type of formatting makes the maintenance of the Emergency Plan document much less labor-intensive for the Emergency Manager, since a needed change in a single policy or procedure requires the rewriting and replacement of only a single sheet (or at most, a couple of sheets) of paper in each manual. Give staff a badge buddy that goes on their lanyard. Put emergency info on the badge buddy—emergency call number of the healthcare institutions or a specific procedure for reporting an ongoing emergency and requesting assistance.

Each copy of the plan should be dated in order to ensure that the reader has access to the most recent version of the instructions, and each should be numbered, so that the Emergency Manager can track each copy and ensure that each copy is maintained with the most current information and instructions. Each page should include a date of creation, and the document tracking page, located in the front of the plan, should describe the date of creation for each page, and also the date of any amendments for that page, along with the reasons for the amendment.

Such measures, although time-consuming, will potentially provide great assistance in any public inquiry, inquest, or other legal action which arises from any emergency event. They provide tremendously valuable transparency as to the precise etiology of any instruction or policy statement, by describing the entire history of the issue, and providing the document with tremendous credibility in the eyes of those conducting the inquiry. It is also wise for the Emergency Manager to create a history file for each page, of the plan, storing copies of each new iteration of each policy or instruction, against a time when the reasons for the creation and use of that policy or instruction may require defense. A sample of the main body of a healthcare-based Emergency Response Plan has been included in Microsoft Word format, on the web page which accompanies this book.

The Annexes

The annexes are secondary plans in their own right, covering a potentially vast variety of subjects and/or situations. The base plan (all hazard) and the annexes (annexes for hazard or incident-specific plans based on your risks as well as functional plans (transportation, etc.)) instructions for particular events which are case specific, such as a specific set of operating instructions and procedures to be used for the evacuation of the hospital, or a response to a mass-casualty event. They may be narrative but are much more likely to be immediately useful if formatted as step-by-step checklists for each type of event.[18] This approach embraces the Six Sigma concept of standardized work as a method of error reduction and provides tremendous consistency, in that every staff member will successfully respond to a given situation, if only they follow the items on the checklist in the correct sequence.

Additionally, the opportunity exists to have staff members literally remove the appropriate annex pages from the binder, placing them on a clipboard and writing on them directly, as each step in the process is completed. By initialing each step and noting the time of completion, the document will probably be admissible in any type of public inquiry, depending, of course, on the rules for each respective jurisdiction. Moreover, by simply having each checklist from each work area forwarded for review once completed, the Emergency Manager has the opportunity to collate these and to document chronologically virtually every step taken within the facility to prepare for response to the emergency in question. The Emergency Manager is also provided with the opportunity to monitor each location for compliance with the specific instructions for the emergency event, and to follow up when noncompliance has been identified. The annexes are relatively inexpensive, usually being produced by photocopying, and can be quickly and easily replaced with new unused copies, following each use.

Increasingly, many healthcare facilities use color coding to describe various types of emergencies. It is even likely, in most facilities, that the subject of a particular annex already possesses a particular color code. This color coding can be taken a step further, in order to make such documents easier for staff to find and access in the Emergency Plan, as per Lean for Healthcare. This might consist of color-coded tabs within the plan binder, and even color-coded pages containing the instructions. While this approach will work well within a facility, one significant drawback is that such codes have only rarely been standardized from one hospital to the next, and only then on a regional basis.[19]

The so-called "clinical" codes, including both adult and pediatric cardiac arrest, are not normally included in the annexes of the Emergency Plan for a healthcare facility. There are generally more than sufficiently

Code	Definition
Code Black	Bomb threat (security incident)
Code Blue	Adult cardiac arrest
Code Brown	Hazardous spill
Code Green	Evacuation
Code Gray	Loss of essential service
Code Orange	External disaster
Code Pink	Pediatric cardiac arrest
Code Purple	Hospital taking/person with weapon
Code Red	Fire
Code White	Violent patient
Code Yellow	Missing patient
Code Amber	Missing infant child

Figure 1.6 Emergency codes

Fire	Mass-Casualty Incident
Severe Weather	Utility Failure (Internal or External)
Bomb Threat	Hazardous Materials Spill
Evacuation	External Air Exclusion
Hostage Incident	Aggressive/Violent Behavior
Missing Patient	Missing/Abducted Infant/Child
Pandemic/Outbreak	Active Shooter/Armed Person
Natural Hazards	Critical Internal System Failure

Figure 1.7 Case-specific annex scenarios

experienced and knowledgeable professionals present to deal with such situations appropriately, and step-by-step instructions would probably be of limited value to those present. Several sample copies of Emergency Plan annexes have been included in Microsoft Word format, on the *web page* which accompanies this book. The situations in Figure 1.7 are those for which the creation of case-specific annexes may be appropriate for a healthcare-based Emergency Plan. The list is by no means exhaustive; every institution and agency has its own needs and experiences and may need to create an annex to deal with that specific event.

Job Action Sheets

These documents, as with the annexes, are generally checklists, although typically highly specific to a particular job or position, such as the Key Role positions in whichever Command and Control model the facility chooses to use. They may also be used to address any seldom used but necessary emergency response task, such as the assembly and activation of the Hospital Command Center from a kit.[20] In each case, the instructions are sequential, specific, and easy to understand. They are intended for short-term use by inexperienced staff who are filling a Key Role on an ad hoc basis for the first time, until relieved by predesignated and trained staff. Talk about the benefits of a Job Action Sheet—disasters are stressful, and people are making decisions and taking actions without full information but based on what they know at the time. It is a reference, and then they know all of the key actions are being done and people can fill in for each other easily if they have their JAS and they have been cross-trained to it. They are of great value for a charge nurse, especially outside of normal business hours.

Job Action Sheets[21] permit a tremendous strength to the organization, in that ad hoc untrained staff may be successfully used successfully (use same word) over the short term, in order to accelerate the activation of the response mechanism outside of normal business hours, an essential ingredient to successful response to an emergency by a hospital. One ordinary staff nurse might fill the role of Incident Manager temporarily, supported by a comprehensive set of instructions, until relieved by the designated Incident Manager, who at 2 a.m. is likely to be responding to the hospital from home. When they arrive, they are greeted by an ad hoc Incident Manager who has begun the steps outlined on the Job Action Sheet, all of which are already documented, and the process of ramping up for response is greatly accelerated.

Job Action Sheets may also be used for guidance through highly necessary but seldom-performed tasks, such as the activation of the Hospital Command Center. By making a correct set of instructions readily available in the Emergency Plan annexes, in the scenario immediately preceding, the designated Incident Manager might very well arrive to find that the Hospital Command Center has already been assembled by support staff with no prior training and is already available for use. Such tools have the potential to greatly accelerate and enhance the response process 24 hours a day. It is possible to create such Job Action Sheets for as many roles as the Emergency Manager has the time (and the energy!) to create; however, what follows in Figures 1.8 and 1.9 are lists of Job Action Sheets which should be considered essential. Several sample copies of Emergency

Incident Manager	Public Information Lead
Safety Officer	Liaison Lead
Operations Chief	Planning Chief
Logistics Chief	Finance Chief
Scribe	Ad hoc Incident Manager

Figure 1.8 Job Action Sheet: roles

Assembly/Activation of Hospital Command Center **Assembly/Activation of Staff Staging Area** **Assembly/Activation of Media Information Center** **Assembly/Activation of Family Information Center** **Assembly/Activation of Temporary Triage Areas** **Assembly/Activation of Temporary Treatment Areas** **Assembly/Activation of Evacuation Resources** **External Emergency Traffic Management Plan**

Figure 1.9 Job Action Sheets: essential tasks

Plan Job Action Sheets in Microsoft Word format have been included on the web page which accompanies this book.

The Appendixes

The appendixes are composed of information which, while highly necessary for the Incident Manager and those in the Hospital Command Center or the Senior Management Team, may not be appropriate for sharing with potentially everyone in the facility or with outside agencies with which copies of the organization's Emergency Plan might be shared. These would include all staff off-duty contact information, including all relevant telephone numbers for each staff member and their work schedule. While such information is essential to have during a crisis, it is also understandable that most staff, particularly those with potential security concerns, would not want this information in general circulation. Similarly, having a detailed contact list for all members of the senior team, the management group, and the incident management team is essential, but should not be generally available to staff. Other numbers which would not be for general distribution would include the "back channel" telephone numbers for other healthcare partners, emergency services, the municipal Emergency Operations Center, or other government agencies. Finally, a contact list for all of the organization's suppliers and contractors, specifying exactly what they provide, purchase order numbers, and 24-hour contact information, is an essential tool for the command center, but not wise to have in general circulation. Under normal circumstances, it is anticipated that the modern facility would store all of this information on computer databases in the Hospital Command Center; however, paper copies of each type of document are still required, against the possibility that the computer system becomes unusable, for any reason.

All of the aforementioned information should be included in the master copy of the Emergency Plan and in all copies of the plan located in the Hospital Command Center. Beyond that, whether or not a particular element of information is appropriate for inclusion in a particular copy of the plan will need to be decided on a case-by-case basis, by the Emergency Manager. Protocols are an important component of an Emergency Plan. Think about COVID-19. Lots of protocols support the COVID-19 base plan, for example, donning and doffing procedures and waste management.

Making Information Accessible

Information, however well intended, is completely useless, unless it is readily accessible by those attempting to find and use it. It is frequently for this reason alone that many Emergency Plans fail, when required. In a healthcare setting, in the middle of a crisis, the person who picks up the Emergency Plan binder to find an element of critical information will frequently discard the binder and improvise, if they cannot find the required information in under about 10 seconds. The information is, in all probability, actually present in the binder, but the combination of old-fashioned narrative writing, difficulty in finding anything, and poor maintenance of the binder often make that information almost impossible to locate quickly.

If the Emergency Manager is to make the Emergency Plan into a document which is perceived by staff to be useful and worthwhile, substantial changes in accessing information will need to take place. It is necessary for the Emergency Manager to put into place and to achieve a goal of permitting any untrained user to access any key element of information within the Emergency Plan in 10 seconds or less. There are many number of traditional approaches to making information accessible which may help to achieve this goal, and also several relatively new ideas. The traditional approaches include numbering pages and tables of contents, as well as the provision of tabs for individual elements of important information.

More recent innovations include the writing philosophy of "one page, one issue," the color-coding of both tabs and, in some cases, pages, and the provision of all associated documents immediately adjacent to the task being described, thereby avoiding any need to search for them.

The division of the Emergency Plan into specific sections, separating the tedious but necessary legal requirements from key information, makes searches both faster and more productive. In some cases, it involves making the associated documents become the actual instructions for action. Finally, since many adults react best during a crisis to visual information, making information accessible may involve the incorporation of flow charts where appropriate. Each of these opportunities will be discussed in detail.

The traditional approach involves making the Emergency Plan less like a binder and more like a book. It provides reference information which the reader has seen before, and already knows how to use, requiring no further training or instruction. This involves the numbering of each page in the plan and the creation of a table of contents, at the front of the binder. This can be further enhanced by the adoption of a writing practice of "one issue, one page," with all of the information for a single issue being presented on a single sheet of paper, with any overflow from the front face being added to the back face of the page. If all the reader wants to know about is who has the authority to activate the Emergency Plan provisions, they can turn directly to that page and access the information, much as they would do in a conventional book. This approach has several advantages; not only can information be accessed quickly and easily by the reader, but when a change in policy or procedure occurs, the Emergency Manager has only to rewrite and replace a single page in each binder, greatly reducing the amount of maintenance required and promoting the currency of information.

The Emergency Plan document may be further enhanced by the division of the Emergency Plan into the main body, containing purely legal and policy information; the annexes, which include case-specific response directions for various issues, such as a missing patient or a bomb threat; role-specific instructions, such as the Job Action Sheets; and task-specific instructions, such as the assembly and activation instructions for a key emergency resource. Finally, it includes the appendixes, which include key elements of information which may be urgently required by some during an emergency response, but which, for reasons of privacy, are not made immediately accessible to all. To illustrate, it is essential, even at 2 a.m., for the Incident Manager to be able to contact the hospital's CEO at home, and this call is welcome, while a call at a similar hour from a disgruntled nurse who hasn't had a meal break would be somewhat less welcome.

The information included in an appendix is always placed in the master copy of the Emergency Plan, and in each copy used in the Hospital Command Center, but its presence in other copies of the plan is determined on a case-by-case basis. This design divides all information into clear categories of "need to know," "nice to know," and "may require." The provision of a glossary of terms and acronyms is intended to clearly express the intended meaning of terms used in the Emergency Plan, thereby eliminating any confusion caused by interdisciplinary jargon disconnects. These design features permit the reader, once the configuration is understood, to narrow their searches and to quickly access only the type of information that they actually require.

The incorporation of annexes which are case specific, role specific, or task specific, provides clear and precise step-by-step instructions to staff in a variety of circumstances. In the case-specific approach, the instructions for action in any specific situation are provided. Most healthcare facilities use this approach for the division of events, but actual approaches vary. To illustrate, if it is 2 a.m. and the fire alarms begin to sound, the new staff nurse or the agency replacement nurse, neither of whom has ever participated in a fire drill in the facility, can quickly access specific instructions for what to do by pulling out the Emergency Plan binder, flipping it open to the tab for "fire," and following the step-by-step instructions from start to finish. Access to the critical information took mere seconds and was almost intuitive in its provision. There is the elimination of waste principle of Lean for Healthcare at its finest; the staff member wasted absolutely no time finding the information, thereby increasing the speed of response to the crisis.

The documentation process can be further enhanced by the use of that particular annex as a worksheet: physically removing the annex from the binder, if necessary, ticking off each item on the list as completed, noting the time of completion, and initialing beside each entry. In this manner, the instruction sheet has become the documentation required, thereby eliminating further searching and waste of time and resources. Upon completion of the emergency, the used copy of the appropriate annex is forwarded to the Emergency Manager for review and archiving, and a new, blank copy replaces it in the binder. The collection and collation of the used annex pages from all affected sites permits the Emergency Manager to develop a comprehensive, step-by-step, chronological narration of the entire organization's response to the emergency, one which is very likely to be admissible in any public inquiry and which is certainly valuable for any internal review. The use of such annex "checklists" for emergency procedures is also an example of "standardized work" in order to eliminate error potential, a key feature of Six Sigma in practice. Record who made what decision when, based on what information at the time.

The role-specific Job Action Sheets can also provide a tremendous advantage in a healthcare setting. Emergencies often occur outside of normal business hours, when the majority of management staff, and presumably most of the predesignated members of the incident management team, are not on site. The site is staffed during these hours largely by staff who, while they may have large amounts of clinical experience, are untrained and inexperienced at managing most types of crises. It is a management responsibility to train staff on what to do and keep annual training records. New staff need to know if their responsibility is matched with authority. This is generally a huge problem. They don't know what they are authorized to do and fear repercussion. Under normal circumstances, such individuals would be forced to simply do what they thought appropriate (called "freelancing") until trained staff arrive and commence the organized response.

By placing role-specific Job Action Sheets in an annex of the Emergency Plan, it becomes possible for untrained staff to simply take those sheets, assign specific acting roles to individuals, and commence the response, well before the arrival of the predesignated staff. Armed with clear, written, step-by-step instructions, the response to the emergency should be well underway, and well documented, when the incident management team members arrive and relieve those who have filled their roles on an ad hoc basis.[22] Such annexes can also serve as a useful memory aid for the predesignated members of the incident management team, particularly if they have not performed their role recently. These documents, when completed, can also be forwarded to the Emergency Manager for archiving and for collation as a part of the documentation of the incident response.

The task-specific Job Action Sheets can also provide a useful tool, particularly during the early stages of any emergency. Tasks which are important, but are only performed occasionally, may be somewhat difficult to perform accurately, particularly under the stressors associated with an emergency response. Such tasks may include, but are not limited to, the assembly of the Hospital Command Center (which may be virtual or a small team only, like an inner circle of the larger command center team) and other emergency-specific work areas, the creation of specific patient-flow patterns in order to manage the emergency more effectively (e.g., suspending outpatient services, suspending elective surgery, and discharging of noncritical in-patients to provide space), placing the facility on external air exclusion to protect against an external event, locking down the facility, creating specific traffic flow and parking patterns on the property in response to an emergency, and establishing a decontamination unit, internal or external to the emergency department, so that you don't contaminate the emergency department.

Armed with appropriate, step-by-step instructions, facility staff, including the incident management team, may perform such tasks with a reasonable degree of safety, since they are referring to a standardized, "no-deviation," set of instructions, developed in advance, and vetted for both safety and clinical appropriateness by other members of staff or outside agencies with real expertise. To illustrate, inexperienced hospital security guards could be quite successful in modifying normal traffic flow to accommodate large numbers of ambulances, particularly if the pattern which they were implementing had been designed in advance, in consultation with local police and Emergency Medical Service (EMS).

As with other types of Job Action Sheets, all steps are documented and signed off, and the annex is simply replaced at the conclusion of the event. Once again, the use of Job Action Sheets represents a good example of the Six Sigma concept of "standardized work" as a method of reduction or outright elimination of errors and creates a level of documented response to an emergency which has never before existed in a healthcare setting. Example templates for various types of Job Action Sheets, in Microsoft Word format, are included on the *web page* which accompanies this book.

Documentation Processes

There is a substantial list of documents which will be required, in order to document the organization's response to any crisis, both correctly and comprehensively. These include the various Job Action Sheets, the role and use of which has already been explained in this chapter. The list also includes a paper mechanism for the tracking of information and resource requests, normally called the information/resource request tracking form. The necessity to create a chronological log of events is addressed through the use of predesigned and printed log sheets, incorporated into their own binder. The completion of these is the responsibility of the Emergency Manager, usually assisted by a Scribe. The Scribe will also require a method for the "minute-ing" of command center meetings, and this will vary from facility to facility, based upon local policies and preferences.

The system will also require a method for reporting current status, normally called a situation report. This document, created by the Incident Manager regularly throughout the response, will be used to share current information and both progress and problems, with response partners both inside and outside of the facility. A method for capturing the information gathered through the debriefing of staff and identification of lessons learned following the event will be required, and the format of this will also be determined locally, according to both policies and preferences. Finally, the Incident Manager collates and summarizes all activities related to the event response in a final report, normally called an after-action report and improvement plan (AAR/IP). While it is expected that such documents will normally be designed by the Emergency Manager in order to satisfy local requirements, example templates for most of these aforementioned documents, in Microsoft Word format, are included on the web page which accompany this book.

Providing Authority

An often-reported issue regarding the failure of Emergency Plans is that staff, while being able to identify which steps were supposed to take place in the response, were unsure whether or not they, as individual staff members, had the authority to implement those steps. This is hardly surprising, since many of the steps outlined in any Emergency Plan are normally beyond the scope of authority for a mid-level manager, much less a front-line staff nurse. Healthcare tends to be a cautious work environment, a necessary feature which has "spilled over" from the clinical arena. In many situations, a staff member who is unsure of what to do may do nothing other than summon help and attempt to deal with the local situation until help arrives. This response has not traditionally been discouraged in the healthcare setting, since some measures, particularly those outlined in an Emergency Plan, may actually have implications involving either finance or liability.

In writing the Emergency Plan, it is essential to ensure that the instructions are crafted in such a manner as to clarify what is to occur and to specifically empower ordinary staff to implement these measures, when it is appropriate to do so. Sometimes, the empowerment is implicit, but often it is not. To illustrate, while no one would dispute a staff member pulling a fire alarm when a fire is discovered, and common sense (it is hoped) would dictate that those patients in the immediate vicinity would be moved to immediate safety, very few would be comfortable to unilaterally decide to evacuate beyond their own floor or to evacuate to a high-risk location, such as an intensive care unit, without specific authorization. At 3 a.m., such specific authorization may not even be in the building! For this reason, it is essential for the Emergency Manager to provide preauthorized specific instructions, including the specification of who has the authority to implement each measure and a specific "trigger point" for its implementation, thereby eliminating the need for inexperienced staff members to decide whether or not the time has come for each measure. The direction *must* be specific; it must specifically provide authority, and it must be unequivocal in its language. To illustrate,

Upon becoming aware of a potential Mass Casualty Incident in progress, any staff member is authorized to implement the first stage of a Mass Casualty Incident response; that implementation will continue but will be reviewed and validated by the first Supervisor to arrive on site.

Peer/Expert Review

It is good practice to create a regular and ongoing process of review, during the creation phase of the Emergency Plan and all of its associated documents. Such review may be peer based, with the addition of "new" eyes often identifying minor errors in the text, potential areas of confusion requiring clarity, or in some cases, even outright errors. Such reviews may be conducted by one workgroup of the Emergency Preparedness Committee exchanging their work with another, or in an innovative approach, by conducting a review using "focus groups" of actual staff. An added benefit of this latter approach is the potential to foster "ownership," and therefore, compliance, with the staff that will have to ultimately use the Emergency Plan.

In some cases, a review by subject-matter "experts" will be required. Hospitals and other healthcare organizations are complex entities, in which knowledge tends to exist in "silos," and where no one, including the Emergency Manager, can possess a comprehensive and detailed knowledge of every operating system, whether clinical, physical, or logistical. This is particularly true in those cases in which clinical issues, building operating systems, telecommunications, or supply chains are involved. Some of these requirements are obvious. To illustrate, it is difficult to imagine creating a set of instructions for the cancellation of elective surgery, without any consultation with the chief of surgery (at minimum) and the operating room charge nurse. Similarly, one could not conceivably provide instructions to staff for the decanting of noncritical in-patients from the hospital without a specific process, approved in advance by the chief of staff and the physician community.

With respect to the physical plant of the hospital, no one understands the operating systems better than the chief engineer; he or she knows specifically what hospital systems can and cannot do, and what the result of any changes to these systems is likely to be. It is essential to access that knowledge through the review process, in order to avoid providing instructions to staff which simply may not work and, in some cases, might even fail catastrophically, if mismanaged. Similar situations also exist for both telecommunications and even supply chain issues. There is little point in providing even the incident management team staff with instructions to contact a particular supplier for a service, if 24-hour contact arrangements with that supplier are not already in place.

Obtaining Approvals

Almost all elements of any Emergency Plan possess the potential for serious implications for the organization which they protect, if used incorrectly or if the information contained is incorrect. The Emergency Plan is intended to provide instructions that are aimed at protecting patients, staff, and the organization against any type of error, which could occur during any emergency. In order to do so, those instructions must be compliant with best practices, policy, and the law and must be performed correctly and must be fully validated, prior to its introduction or use.

From the perspective of potential liability, it is essential that all elements of the Emergency Plan be reviewed by, and approved by, the Senior Management Team of the organization, prior to implementation. In some organizations, this may simply involve providing the opportunity to read over the completed document in "draft" form and to offer both factual corrections and suggestions for improvement. In other organizations, it may actually involve a process of presentations to the senior team by the Emergency Manager. Finally, it may involve the need for a review by corporate legal counsel, in order to ensure compliance with both laws and regulations. Get stakeholder feedback; ask people if it works? Does it make sense? Is this how we operate? Integrate the feedback. Do a structured walk-through of your plan's concepts. List the strategic decisions that management has to make and build into the plan (outline the impacts).

In all cases, the entire approval process must be meticulously documented by the Emergency Manager. The dates of delivery and return of the entire document, or sections of the document, who they were delivered to, and what specific feedback was provided must be included in the documentation. Any discussions, including telephone conversations, should be documented, and any meetings should be minuted. The contents of any presentations to senior staff should also be archived. By doing so, the process for the review and approval of the Emergency Plan remains completely transparent and very difficult to criticize in any future public inquiry or other legal action.

In all cases, the review and consultation process should be meticulously documented. Records must be maintained of every review process, every discussion, and every meeting. All correspondence regarding this review process should also be archived by the Emergency Manager. These measures provide a necessary and complete transparency in the plan creation process. It is also not uncommon for the etiology of a particular element of instructions or work direction to become the subject of discussion at any future public inquiry or other legal action. When such documentation is absent and cannot be introduced, the process of creation of the instruction or work direction can potentially become the subject of speculation—an entirely undesirable outcome which good documentation prevents. Give people electronic copies. Put EM manuals in strategic locations for easy access during an emergency. Create an Emergencies Cart—with the plan and emergency supplies—and locate these manuals throughout the facility. Develop and have in place a system with which staff will easily know which rooms have already been evacuated.

Conclusion

The information included in this chapter, including both the proposed sections and the approach to the structuring and provision of access to information, is innovative. While the sections include some of the best features of older-style Emergency Plans, some elements are completely new to emergency preparedness in healthcare settings. The incorporation of essential principles of mainstream management practices such as Lean, Six Sigma, and Project Management is intended to create a document which is better understood and, therefore, more valued by the management team than has traditionally been the case. The ease-of-use features, including making information easy to find and providing instructions which are immediately clear and straightforward, will also ensure that front-line staff value and use the plan, rather than "freelancing" because they cannot easily find the information that they need. The practices outlined in this chapter should also provide the healthcare-based Emergency Manager with increased credibility among the management team of the hospital or other healthcare organization, and among front-line healthcare staff in general.

Student Projects

Student Project #1

Select a single adverse event with a potential to occur within a healthcare setting. Research the nature of the event appropriately and identify any critical systems which would be affected by the event. Consult with those responsible for the critical systems in question, in order to fully understand the impacts and the response requirements. Now create a checklist tool to respond to this event, for use by a new manager with minimal familiarity with the building or the systems in question. Create a report to accompany the checklist, describing the process of creation and the process of consultation and citing the appropriate references, in order to demonstrate that the appropriate research and consultation have occurred.

Student Project #2

Select a single, emergency-specific resource, such as the Hospital Command Center, the media information center, the family information center, and staff staging area, which is not normally in operation within the facility. Review in detail the process for the creation of that resource, including primary and backup locations, physical layout, resource requirements, staffing, and activation procedures. Now create a step-by-step checklist for the activation of that resource for use by a new manager with minimal familiarity with the building and its operating systems. Ensure that you include specific detail on the location of all required resources, and how to obtain their use, including access outside of normal business hours. Create a report to accompany the checklist, describing the process of creation and the process of consultation and citing the appropriate references, in order to demonstrate that the appropriate research and consultation have occurred.

Test Your Knowledge

Take your time. Read each question carefully and select the *most correct* answer for each. The correct answers appear at the end of the section.

If you score less than 80 percent (8 correct answers) you should reread this chapter.

1. A segment of the Emergency Plan which contains case-specific instructions for dealing with a specific type of emergency is called:

   (a) The main body
   (b) An appendix
   (c) A Job Action Sheet
   (d) An annex

2. A segment of the Emergency Plan which contains information which is not for general distribution, such as home telephone numbers for senior staff, is called:

   (a) The main body
   (b) An appendix
   (c) A Job Action Sheet
   (d) An annex

3. A segment of the Emergency Plan which contains specific instructions for the activation of a Key Role position or for the assembly of an emergency-specific resource, such as the command center, is called:

   (a) The main body
   (b) An appendix
   (c) A Job Action Sheet
   (d) An annex

4. A formal statement outlining the scope of the Emergency Plan, describing the legal authority for the plan, or outlining authority to activate the Emergency Plan, would be contained in:

   (a) The main body
   (b) An appendix
   (c) A Job Action Sheet
   (d) An annex

5. A critical principle of Emergency Plan design which reflects the philosophy of the Lean for Healthcare system is:

   (a) Ease of access to information for the user
   (b) Keeping language simple for the user
   (c) Standardizing work for the user
   (d) Both (b) and (c)

6. Six Sigma is a management system which is primarily designed to:

   (a) Define responsibilities
   (b) Eliminate errors wherever possible
   (c) Define legal responsibilities
   (d) Reduce the number of plan copies in circulation

7. The widespread use of comprehensive checklists in the Emergency Plan is an application of the Six Sigma principle of:

   (a) Providing clear instructions
   (b) Comprehensive simplicity
   (c) Standardized work
   (d) High-quality documentation

8. One of the strengths of the Job Action Sheet in an Emergency Plan for a healthcare setting is the ability for staff with minimal training to begin to activate the Emergency Plan:

   (a) Outside of normal business hours
   (b) When specially trained staff are not immediately available
   (c) During the business day when leaders are busy
   (d) Both (a) and (b)

9. The segment of the Emergency Plan which clearly defines what the plan is intended to be used for and what it is not intended to be used for is called the:

   (a) Statement of scope
   (b) Statement of authority
   (c) Authority to activate statement
   (d) Spending authority statement

10. In order to be considered current in most jurisdictions, an Emergency Plan document should be reviewed following each emergency event or exercise, and revised at least:

(a) Every six months
(b) Annually
(c) Every two years
(d) Every five years

Answers

1. (d)   2. (b)   3. (c)   4. (a)   5. (a)
6. (b)   7. (c)   8. (d)   9. (a)   10. (c)

Additional Reading

The author recommends the following exceptionally good titles as supplemental readings, which will help to enhance the student's knowledge of those topics covered in this chapter:

Hospital Emergency Operations Plan. 2013. New York, NY: University Hospital of Brooklyn, .pdf document. http://training.fema.gov/EMIWeb/edu/docs/nimsc2/NIMS%20-%20Lab%2010%20-%20Handout%20 10-13-Hospital%20EOP.pdf (accessed January 31, 2014).

Rittman, S.J., K.I. Shoaf, and A. Dorian. 2005. *Writing A Disaster Plan: A Guide For Health Departments*. UCLA Centre for Public Health and Disasters, .pdf document. ftp://ftp.cdc.gov/pub/phlpprep/Legal%20Preparedness%20for% 20Pandemic%20Flu/8.0%20-%20Non-Governmental%20Materials/ 8.6%20Writing%20a%20Disaster%20Plan%20-%20UCLA.pdf (accessed January 31, 2014).

Shirley, D. 2011. *Project Management for Healthcare*. Boca Raton, FL: CRC Press.

Sorensen, B.S., R.D. Zane, B.E. Wante, M.B. Rao, M. Bortolin, and G. Rockenschaub. 2011. *Hospital Emergency Response Checklist: An All-Hazards Tool for Hospital Administrators and Emergency Managers*. World Health Organization, .pdf document. www.euro.who.int/__data/assets/pdf_file/ 0020/148214/e95978.pdf (accessed January 31, 2014).

CHAPTER 2

The Emergency Preparedness Committee

Introduction

The creation of an Emergency Management program is a huge task, one that the Emergency Manager should not have to complete alone. In any hospital or other healthcare facility, there exists a vast array of expertise regarding most parts of the facility's operation, and the Emergency Manager must be able to harness this resource, in order to provide both an Emergency Plan and associated programs which can be operationalized and which meet the specific needs of that facility. The Emergency Preparedness Committee is the essential tool for the marshaling of expertise and the application of that expertise to the organization's Emergency Plan and the associated procedures and training efforts. While such an entity is clearly valuable, it is not without its challenges. Conflicting priorities can make member recruitment/retention difficult, and the activities of the committee may not be seen as a priority by other members of the management group.

The Emergency Manager will be required to be a work director, a motivator, a conflict mediator, and a coach, and all for committee members who only report directly to the Emergency Manager on this single issue.[1] Some may be in entirely different lines of authority, and some may even possess more day-to-day authority than the Emergency Manager. It is the job of the Emergency Manager to create a team which not only has the appropriate expertise, but which also remains committed, engaged, and productive, for without the active efforts of the Emergency Manager, the very continuation of the Emergency Preparedness Committee can be a challenge. The Emergency Manager must be both a team player and an excellent manager, one with excellent people skills and creative skills.[2]

Learning Objectives

On completion of this chapter, the student should be able to describe the step-by-step process for the creation of an Emergency Preparedness Committee for a healthcare facility. The student should be familiar with the processes of recruitment and selection of committee members, as well as the potential obstacles which may need to be overcome as part of the recruitment process. The student will be able to describe, in detail, the activities carried out by the committee members, both individually and in groups, and how to monitor those activities, provide feedback, and motivate committee members to produce the best possible work.

Building the Committee

The biggest single challenge to the creation and maintenance of an Emergency Preparedness Committee is often the ability to attract sufficient numbers of individuals with the appropriate skill sets and organizational knowledge from the workforce. A broad skill set is required, including program management, research, policy creation, and manual dynamics.[3] In addition, the committee will need to be representative of all departments operating in the facility—at a minimum, organizational leadership, legal, nursing, security, human resources, chaplaincy, environmental health, security, laboratories, emergency department, public affairs, occupational health and safety, infection control, and engineering.[4] In ideal circumstances, the physician group would also be represented and particularly the consultant/specialist group, although these are typically the most difficult groups to obtain representation from. In addition, past experience has taught that the inclusion and participation of any unions representing staff are also highly desirable.

There are several challenges that need to be overcome. The first of these is that the people who the Emergency Manager is attempting to attract to committee membership are normally busy people, usually with their own operating priorities, time demands, and specific areas of interest. Participation in another committee may require considerable powers of persuasion on the part of the Emergency Manager. One of the best methods for overcoming this reluctance is to raise the public profile of participation in the committee. Sharing regular committee status reports, such as meeting minutes and outlining the contributions of individual members, with senior management, can often have this result. Public acknowledgment of specific contributions can also produce a similar result.

Another challenge is that, however worthwhile the work of the Emergency Preparedness Committee might be, it is likely to be perceived as a secondary consideration, after the core business of healthcare. Healthcare facilities are a busy environment, with both high demands for services and limited resources with which to provide them. Any prospective committee members are likely to report to someone else, and that person is quite likely to be operating on a daily basis with a workload that exceeds available resources. Any request to "borrow" staff for any activity, and particularly for an activity not perceived as being an essential part of the "core business," is likely to be met with a great deal of resistance. In this case, persuasion may consist of outlining the contributions of the department in question to an essential process. It may also be possible to persuade participation on the basis of staff development. At an absolute minimum, the wise Emergency Manager will be fastidiously respectful of the conflicting time demands placed on each committee member, ensuring that meetings are actually productive, that they finish on time, and that no unreasonable or excessive demands are placed upon the members' time.

The process of recruitment may begin with a general call for volunteers. If this approach works, the Emergency Manager may only need to pick from among the volunteers, supplementing them with specifically requested expertise resources, requested by the appropriate manager. If this is not acceptable, the Emergency Manager may need to resort to formal requests from the managers of staff representing the required areas of expertise and skill sets. Neither of these is ideal, but it is an inescapable fact that Emergency Managers in a healthcare setting are unlikely to have much staff reporting directly to them and are required to depend on the use of staff who normally report to other managers who have differing priorities.

It can also be useful to carefully schedule meetings, ensuring not to place too high a demand upon the membership, and to provide advance estimates of the time demands on individual members. The creation and circulation of a formal meeting agenda and meeting minutes may also aid others in seeing the value of the work being performed. Finally, committing to the actual terms of service for committee members, with defined terms of office, such as one or two years, may help to ease concerns among managers. That being said, the Emergency Manager must take care to rotate committee members' service in groups, so that the continuity of the committee's work is not lost.

It is essential that such a committee has the correct composition. Simply having the right knowledge and skills is insufficient; people have to *want* to be there, and they have to *want* to work together! Anything less leads to substandard performance on assignments, disruptive behavior in meetings, or even absenteeism. Also undesirable are the "resume surfers"—that group of employees who move from project to project, attempting to build their resumes, but not making any particular contribution to the committee. While such a practice may very well be an excellent "selling point" for recruiting committee members, one does *not* want members for whom this is the sole reason for membership. Those chosen for the committee must believe that the work of the committee is important and that they are capable of making a significant contribution to that work. The Emergency Manager needs people who, to sum it up, actually *want* to be there!

The Role of the "Champion"

Most Senior Management Teams are responsive to the presentation of good ideas. That being said, competing priorities, and limited time and funding in a healthcare system, will generally lead to the development of an "annual priorities" list for the organization, a list which Emergency Management often has difficulty in achieving a place on. Many on the Senior Management Team, like the rest of the management structure, typically tend to see Emergency Management as being "outside of the core businesses" of the organization and, as a result, rarely give it much priority. A culture has evolved in many healthcare settings in which Emergency

Management will normally only receive serious consideration either in the months before an accreditation visit or in the months following a disaster. The unfortunate presence of such "windows" can make Emergency Management generally a difficult "sell," particularly if approval or funding is required for some type of activity.

The good news is that members of the Senior Management Team of a healthcare organization almost always have their own priorities and "pet" projects. They typically talk about these issues at virtually every meeting and attempt to boost support for the projects among other members of the team. There may even be a system of "quid pro quo" operating, in which each member of the management team will support the project of another, as long as that support is reciprocated for their own project. The challenge is to find one's way into this system. This can often be accomplished through the recruitment of a member of the Senior Management Team to the Emergency Preparedness Committee. To use a healthcare analogy, if one can "infect" a single member of the Senior Management Team with interest and enthusiasm about this topic, he or she may very well be able to "infect" others on the team! It is also in their interest for the Emergency Preparedness Committee to succeed; if it does not, there is a very real possibility (at least in their minds) that, since they are a significant leader in the organization, the stalling or outright failure of the committee might even reflect negatively on them.

Just as in the Six Sigma model, the recruitment of a "champion"[5] from among the Senior Management Team can greatly help to enhance the Emergency Management process, as well as the status and contributions of the Emergency Preparedness Committee. Just as a Six Sigma champion is responsible for the implementation of that process and its practices across an organization in an integrated manner, a "champion" for the Emergency Preparedness Committee may very well be able to achieve the same result. To do so, the "champion" will need to be convinced that the information and requests being generated by the committee have evolved from the old-fashioned "just-in-case" risk management approach to the result of actual research and analysis, based upon recognizable processes, such as Six Sigma and Lean for Healthcare.

The "champion" will also need to be convinced that the projects being proposed will be subject to formal project plans and that they are intended to protect against loss and liability, preserve the public image of the facility, and demonstrate due diligence. In summary, they need to be composed entirely of methods that the "champion" can recognize and respect. This approach will not only satisfy the "champions" but also provide them with the precise material which they require in order to "sell" the committee's requests and projects to the balance of the Senior Management Team and other critical hospital committees.

To illustrate, the Emergency Preparedness Committee is recommending a significant change to the fundamental process of patient flow during a disaster. This might normally meet with tremendous resistance from the physician community and the chief nursing executive, particularly in the context of "we think that this might work better." Now, as an alternative, the same proposal is presented, this time based upon Six Sigma-driven problem analysis or root cause analysis,[7] which identifies the significant potential for errors, or outright flaws, resulting in potential liability exposures, and subjected to a Value Stream Map from Lean for Healthcare,[8] in order to identify areas for improvement. The research and analysis were performed by an interdisciplinary team, which included both physician and nursing representatives. The report is then submitted along with a formal project plan for implementation;[9] the result is very likely to be quite different. A "champion" can be an invaluable member of the Emergency Preparedness Committee, and an essential part of the Emergency Management process, as long as they can be supported by the tools which they need to do their job.

Keeping Things Organized

This is a good time to recall the project plan, which was described elsewhere in this work. The creation of an Emergency Response Plan is a daunting task, even for a committee. With so many planning tasks to be performed, it is a common problem for individuals or subgroups of the committee to become distracted or to lose their way. Such issues, while common, can be overcome with advance planning by the Emergency Manager. The entire emergency preparedness process has evolved tremendously, well beyond the traditional response plan, and should, if it is to be effective, reach into all aspects of Emergency Management, creating a Strategic Emergency Management Plan.

Emergency Management Continuum

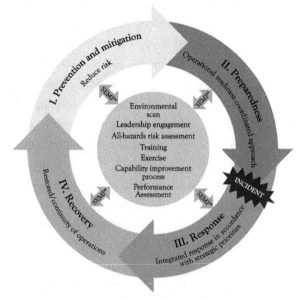

Figure 2.1 As Emergency Management becomes more complex, so does the job of the facility's Emergency Preparedness Committee

*SEMP = Strategic Emergency Management Plan

Wherever possible, the skill set and knowledge which brought the individual members to the Emergency Preparedness Committee in the first place will probably determine workgroups and task assignments. It only makes sense for the Emergency Manager to exploit fully those strengths which they have worked so hard to add to the committee. If the Emergency Manager has obtained a decision from the organization to use the incident management system Command and Control model, this provides an opportunity to apply the same model to the entire planning process.

Consider which Command and Control model will be used within your organization. Command and Control models are originally intended to manage an emergency. However, what is less recognized is that a Command and Control model can also make a highly effective framework for the planning process, whichever model has been chosen. The incident management system model, for example, is an excellent framework not only for controlling an incident but also for preincident planning. The use of the Command and Control model for planning can also provide committee members with valuable skills and experience in its use, which are then directly transferrable to real-life incident management.

The Key Roles of the model are an excellent place to start. Each of these is intended to address one major issue that every organization, regardless of their role or core business, must at least consider during the response to a crisis. With that in mind, it seems only logical to divide planning responsibilities according to these major issues. As a result, a well-organized committee might very well end up with subcommittees that address Command, Public Information, Liaison, Safety, Operations, Planning, Logistics, and Finance aspects of the Emergency Response Plan.[10] In such an arrangement, the majority of the provisions for that aspect of the plan will be created directly by those who are most likely to have to implement them in a real-life event.

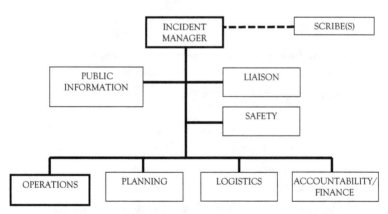

Figure 2.2 One possible approach to committee organization

To illustrate, a safety subcommittee might well consist of those recruited from both Infection Control and Occupational Health and Safety because these are the individuals most likely to be involved in the safety function during a real event. This approach makes perfect sense because the individuals doing the planning already have the required expertise and the clearest and most comprehensive understanding of the associated issues arising in this role. There are those who advocate the preassignment of all incident management system Key Roles to those who perform a similar function on a daily basis; this is just another example of such an approach in actual operation.

On a similar note, it may be appropriate to subdivide the case-specific annexes into subgroups of the committee which are staffed by those with real expertise in the subject matter. In this manner, the work and instructions are similar to be generated by those who best understand the issues, what is possible, and what is not. To illustrate this in operation, a case-specific annex intended to provide instructions for dealing with a hazardous materials spill on the facility's premises might very well be assigned to a workgroup or subcommittee consisting of Occupational Health and Safety, Laboratories, Environmental Services, and Engineering. Once again, these are the groups with the greatest vested interest in how this annex is crafted and in how well it will work.

Maintaining Focus

One of the challenges which can be associated with the creation of an Emergency Response Plan by a committee is that almost everyone who is on such a committee is very likely to have their own agenda for how they want the plan to work and to look. This pursuit of individual priorities can often distract or confuse committee members and has the potential to greatly slow the progress of the plan. Much of this can be avoided in advance through the advance preparations of the Emergency Manager. It can consist of process-related measures for subcommittee meetings, such as well-organized, publicized, and monitored timelines for the completion of each step in the process of plan creation. The project plan itself has a critical path and benchmarks for completion, and each subordinate step in that process should also have specific timelines of its own, with accountability for failure to meet the objectives. This can serve to make other subcommittee members less likely to quietly tolerate behaviors that waste work time.

Measures related to meeting organization, such as the keeping of meeting minutes or specifically limiting the time allocated to each speaker during a discussion, thereby avoiding the problem of any individual monopolizing a meeting in order to persuade, and in some cases, even browbeat, other members to support their agenda, can also be useful. The Emergency Manager may not be able to attend each and every sub-committee meeting (although regular visits are a good idea!); they can and should preappoint subcommittee chairs who they know to have a strong enough personality to control any disruptive behavior. The Emergency Manager must also be prepared to take decisive action, such as the removal of a committee member, if they demonstrate a consistent or repeated pattern of disruptive behavior that is slowing the process of plan creation.

A Well-Functioning Committee

Despite the obvious challenges which are inherent in committee work in general, there are also clear signs that the committee is doing its job effectively. For an effective manager of any type, the health of any committee should be relatively easy to judge objectively through the use of such signs. These are signs that the Emergency Manager should look for and should monitor on an ongoing basis, in order to identify and fix problems early and to ensure that the committee can continue to function effectively.

Figure 2.3 An effective Emergency Preparedness Committee. Note the diverse and representative membership

The first of these signs is that the purpose of the committee is clear to all. Does everyone on the committee understand the purpose of the committee clearly? Do others, not directly involved in the committee, understand its purpose, or is negative speculation about its purpose or activities present? These may be signs that the committee members have not received sufficient orientation from the Emergency Manager or that the work of the committee is not understood or valued by others. Such comments by others within the workplace may lead members of the Emergency Preparedness Committee to conclude that their work is not being understood or valued by their coworkers. Committee members are human, and everyone involved would prefer to be involved with a successful project.

The next of these signs is careful time control. As already stated, the committee members are all busy people with competing time demands, and no one likes to see their time wasted. Starting and finishing meetings on time shows that the Emergency Manager understands and respects the pressures placed upon committee members by the ever-present time constraints. The development of and adherence to the project plan, including specific timelines and time-sensitive milestones, is also important; they help the Emergency Manager to monitor progress effectively and permit individual committee members to see those specific areas of progress that are occurring as a result of the committee's work. Therefore, they are more likely to continue to perceive the work of the committee as valuable and worthy of their time away from addressing other conflicting demands.

Good communication and mutual sensitivity among members are also important. Communication between committee members must not only be effective but also remain respectful and inclusive. While the formation of individually tasked workgroups is an essential part of the process, it must not become a basis for the formation of factions or "cliques" within the committee. If a member, who is not on the evacuation subcommittee, happens to bring forward an idea, concern, or perspective regarding evacuation, this should receive the same attention as it would if it had been raised by a member of that subcommittee.

The Emergency Manager should ensure that, wherever possible, the committee functions at all times in an informal and relaxed atmosphere. There are timelines, of course, and these need to be met, but the work of the committee must remain pleasant for the members. Bear in mind that these individuals are generally under constant time pressure and may even work in environments in which rigid discipline and hierarchies are the norm. Such pressurized environments often generate dissatisfied employees. Committee work needs to be done, but it also needs to remain a pleasant experience for the participants. Excessive formality and regimentation can cause committee members to view attendance at meetings as something to be avoided.

Good preparation for each meeting on the part of the chair and members is essential. It basically comes back to the concept of mutual respect for each other and for each other's limited time. Each meeting should have a formal agenda, which should be created and circulated in advance. Individual members should have the ability to add items to that agenda. Specific times should be allocated for each agenda item. The Emergency Manager should ensure that whoever is dealing with each agenda item is contacted in advance and is ready to proceed. This includes the Emergency Manager! People tend to see disorganized meetings with unprepared presenters as largely a waste of their time. If the problem becomes persistent, they will often begin to seek reasons to discontinue their participation in the committee entirely.

The members of the committee must remain interested and committed to the committee's work and objectives. There is little point, or value, to populating a seat at the meeting with someone who sees no value in what is occurring and who would really rather be somewhere else, working on something which they find more interesting. There are those who attend meetings and never make a contribution of any type; they may lack confidence or feel that they have nothing to contribute, or they may be either using committee membership as a means of obtaining a "break" during a hectic schedule, or simply one of those people who like to add committee memberships, in order to "pad" their resumes, but who have no real interest or commitment to the work of the committee. Such people tend to frustrate the more committed members of the committee and, in extreme cases, may even become disruptive for the purpose of entertaining themselves, if they become bored. As a result, the membership of such individuals in the Emergency Preparedness Committee should be avoided, wherever possible.

An effective committee keeps and circulates meeting minutes that are both complete and concise. The minutes can provide a valuable source of information regarding the activities of the committee. Such minutes can not only demonstrate the positive progress being made but also be used to showcase any outstanding contributions by individual committee members. This reinforces for the management team the positive value of the committee's activities and may also raise the profile of Emergency Management as a management priority. It can provide a level of transparency that has the potential to raise the committee's contributions in the estimation of the management team. It can also help to raise the profiles of individual committee members, thereby reinforcing the positive effects of committee participation. It is often insufficient to simply do good work…one must be seen to be doing good work!

An effective Emergency Preparedness Committee provides new opportunities to learn and exercise skills that have the potential to lead to career advancement for members. Such courses should include not only traditional Emergency Management topics, but also essential supporting skills with application to their daily work, such as Lean, Six Sigma, Project Management, and Applied Research Methodology. These may include the facilitation of provincial, state, and local course training, FEMA distance education courses, or even diploma or degree programs.

Periodic frank and open assessments of the performance of both the committee itself and of individual members will permit the Emergency Manager to build a base of support among the membership, and, with appropriate recognition of the contributions of individual members and subcommittees, all involved receive positive reinforcement and understand that their contributions are being both recognized and appreciated. At the same time, such transparency within the committee's reporting to the Senior Management Team ensures that the work of the committee is accepted and contributes to the organization which is increasingly seen as valuable.

Conclusion

The creation and operation of an Emergency Preparedness Committee can be a significant challenge for any Emergency Manager operating in a healthcare setting. When operated correctly, it can become a recognized pool of residential expertise in the creation of the Emergency Plan, the acquisition of emergency response resources, the training of staff, and, in essence, all things related to emergency preparedness. When operated incorrectly or when the support of the Senior Management Team is lacking, it can become yet another temporary committee, struck a few months prior to accreditation, and then immediately disbanded, losing all of the expertise which had been developed. To achieve the goal of a respected, permanent committee producing work that is valued, the Emergency Manager must become a highly effective project planner, a leader, a mentor, a coach, and a mediator. Skills in the areas of Project Management, research, managing people, and even conflict resolution will be required. With these realities in mind, when formulated and operated correctly, an Emergency Preparedness Committee can become an invaluable resource, not only for the Emergency Manager, but for the organization itself.

Student Projects

Student Project #1

Create a document describing the process of selection and recruitment of Emergency Preparedness Committee members for a new committee to be established at your facility. Outline the measures which will need to be taken in advance to ensure the success of the committee. Describe the entire recruitment and selection process, up to the inaugural meeting, using the techniques of Project Management. Be sure to cite and reference appropriately, in order to demonstrate that sufficient relevant research has occurred on this project.

Student Project #2

Create a formal Project Management plan for the creation, recruitment, and inaugural meeting of a new Emergency Preparedness Committee for your facility. Identify potential candidates, according to both position in the organization and desirable skill sets. Describe any potential problems which are likely to occur in the process of creation and provide at least one method of response to each potential problem identified. Be sure to cite and reference appropriately, in order to demonstrate that sufficient relevant research has occurred on this project.

Test Your Knowledge

Take your time. Read each question carefully and select the *most correct* answer for each. The correct answers appear at the end of the section. If you score less than 80 percent (8 correct answers) you should reread this chapter.

1. An Emergency Preparedness Committee is an essential tool to assist the Emergency Manager in obtaining specific types of expertise related to the facility and its work and:

   (a) Permitting input into the process of Emergency Plan creation
   (b) Obtaining champions for the Emergency Plan
   (c) Addressing specific issues relating to the facility and its work
   (d) All of the above

2. It is essential to attempt to recruit at least one committee member from among the senior management group, as this person may:

   (a) Fill the role of champion for the committee's activities
   (b) Provide detailed explanations of policies to committee members
   (c) Provide ongoing work direction from senior management
   (d) All of the above

3. One way to attract candidates to committee membership is through:

   (a) Turning committee membership into a high-visibility showcase of skills
   (b) Appealing to the egos of candidates
   (c) Requesting managers to assign staff to the roles
   (d) Both (b) and (c)

4. In order to convince managers to permit candidates to participate in the committee, the Emergency Manager will need to be:

   (a) Very persuasive
   (b) Always respectful of the existing time and work demands on the employee

(c) Prepared to share credit for accomplishments with the manager

(d) All of the above

5. In order to ensure that the committee remains focused on the project, it will be necessary for the Emergency Manager to:

   (a) Have an advance plan and objectives for each meeting

   (b) Exert control to keep the members focused on the actual agenda

   (c) Politely but firmly put an end to any disruptive behavior

   (d) All of the above

6. One of the best methods for the Emergency Manager to showcase the skills and contributions of individual committee members is to:

   (a) Have regular meetings with the member's manager

   (b) Share copies of meeting minutes with senior management regularly

   (c) Create a committee newsletter

   (d) All of the above

7. Breaking the committee into job-specific workgroups permits the Emergency Manager to:

   (a) Isolate those who may be causing disruptions

   (b) Focus the member's known expertise on specific tasks

   (c) Permit key elements of the project to occur concurrently

   (d) Both (b) and (c)

8. One way to ensure the completion of committee projects on time is through the use by the Emergency Manager of:

   (a) Clearly understood and monitored timelines for each element of the project

   (b) Checking on project progress on a daily basis

   (c) Regular reminder e-mails to committee members

   (d) Both (b) and (c)

9. The most effective method of obtaining optimum performance from committee members is through the use of:

   (a) Regular positive reinforcement, feedback, and coaching

   (b) Regular monitoring with reports to the member's regular manager

(c) Signed memoranda of understanding

(d) All of the above

10. The easiest method of ensuring the continued participation of committee members is for the Emergency Manager to:

(a) Permit committee members to work on other projects on committee time

(b) Publicly acknowledge each member's accomplishments and contributions

(c) Make the committee member feel that their work is valued

(d) Both (b) and (c)

Answers

1. (d)   2. (a)   3. (a)   4. (b)   5. (d)

6. (b)   7. (d)   8. (a)   9. (a)   10. (d)

Additional Reading

The author recommends the following exceptionally good titles as supplemental readings, which will help to enhance the student's knowledge of those topics covered in this chapter:

Barr, J. and L. Dowding. 2015. *Leadership in Health Care*. London: Sage Publications.

Etter, R. and P.A. Robinson. 2010. *Writing and Designing Manuals, 3rd ed.* Boca Raton, FL: CRC Press.

Joint Commission Resources Inc. 2002. *Guide to Emergency Management Planning in Health Care*. Oakbrook Terrace, IL: Joint Commission Resources.

Lowenthal, J.N. 2002. *Six SIGMA Project Management: A Pocket Guide*. Milwaukee, WI: ASQ Quality Press.

Norman, S. and J. Stuart-Black. 2006. *Health Emergency Planning: A Handbook for Practitioners*. Norwich, UK: TSO Publications.

Reilly, M.J. and D.S. Markenson. 2011. *Health Care Emergency Management: Principles and Practise*. Sudbury Mass: Jones and Bartlett Learning.

Veneema, T.G. 2013. *Disaster Nursing and Emergency Preparedness for Chemical, Biological, and Radiological Terrorism and Other Hazards*. New York, NY: Springer Pub. Co.

CHAPTER 3

Coordinated Interfacility Planning

Introduction

Communitywide or regional emergencies can often pose significant challenges for healthcare institutions. Hospitals and long-term care facilities which may not have significant contact on a daily basis or which, in some cases, actually view one another as competitors will all have to shoulder the burden of disaster response. They may do this in isolation from their neighbors, much as some of them do every day, but the response will be much better for all concerned if they can work together. Unfortunately, there are often significant barriers to coordinated responses. Some of these may have occurred deliberately, as with the tendency to view other hospitals as competitors.[1] It can also be quite accidental because when advance planning and preparedness activities occur in a "silo," hospitals often make conscious choices, such as communications technologies, which actually make work easier within their own facility, but which also make coordinated response more difficult.

This chapter will focus on the ideal of coordinated responses to disasters by all of the healthcare facilities within a community. It will also examine those issues which can create potential barriers to coordinated response and how and why these barriers can sometimes occur. The chapter will examine strategies used by the Emergency Manager to overcome such barriers as a part of day-to-day practice. Finally, it will examine some best practices, aimed at ensuring that healthcare providers can coordinate their activities quickly and easily to respond to a disaster, when this is required.

Learning Objectives

On completion of this chapter, the student should be able to describe the advantages of interfacility coordination by healthcare facilities for the purpose of disaster response. The student should also be able to describe the potential barriers to interfacility coordination, as well as effective strategies which may be available to overcome such barriers, including day-to-day practices which can be incorporated into the practice of Emergency Management within a healthcare facility.

Working With Your Neighbors

The first steps toward working with other healthcare facilities in the region is getting to know them. That may sound strange; no doubt most people probably believe that either the other facility's resources are obvious or that they can't be too different from one facility to the next. In fact, one facility probably knows a lot less about neighboring facilities than they think, and differences in philosophy and methodology which are not immediately obvious may nevertheless be profound. Working together to address disaster response, with formal coordination arrangements, is a highly desirable outcome, but not one which is ordinarily easy to achieve. In order to achieve this goal, a certain amount of simple will is desired; there are attitudes, philosophies, and conflicting priorities to be overcome, and there are also some barriers, which are not inconsiderable, which will also need to be overcome by the Emergency Managers of all of the participating facilities.

Potential Barriers

Attitudes and Philosophies

There are two key problems with respect to attitude which are encountered almost universally by Emergency Managers, regardless of what setting they are practicing in. The first of these is that Emergency Management activities are less important than the core business of the organization. The second is that the required resources are already in place, negating any need for further action. Many Chief Executive Officers in healthcare fail to see the direct connection between business continuity, a process which most understand, and Emergency Management, which most, unfortunately, do not.

Many CEOs see the building of the business, in this case, a hospital, as being their core concern in an often intensely competitive environment. Indeed, there are some, including those in Britain's National Health Service, who believe that the competitive environment may actually improve service quality.[2] While the development of a hospital which is resilient—that is to say that it can quickly and effectively recover from any impact from an adverse event and continue to provide quality service—should be a priority, many CEOs become distracted by the competition itself. It has even been said that among CEOs, resiliency will not be considered important until it can be shown to be a competitive advantage!

Another challenge is the troublesome combination of competing demands and limited resources. A healthcare facility is a business, like any other, and money is important. Moreover, medical technologies are in a constant state of flux; each new iteration of technology, an MRI Scanner, for example, typically has an obsolescence window of around five to seven years, and the physical plant which houses these technologies typically has a similar lifespan.[3] Such technological change devours a good deal of a healthcare facility's available resources, but without them, the facility loses its "state-of-the-art" designation, and therefore, some of its competitive edge.

Each department is going to have its own ideas, programs, and both physical and staffing requirements. The leadership of each department puts a great deal of time and effort into obtaining what their department requires, with meticulously researched and written proposals and business plans, and presentations to senior management, often supported by vendors with a vested interest in selling their product. Those needs are often seen as immediate, and many department heads, upon successfully inaugurating a new technology in their department, immediately commence the next five-year plan for its replacement.

When faced with this type of challenge, the healthcare-based Emergency Manager, whose presentation skills were, at least at one time, "we should probably do this…just in case this occurs," has a real problem. When facing such stridently competing priorities for limited resources, the CEO is very likely to develop an attitude of "why should I use limited and much-needed resources to address something which, frankly, might never happen?" Indeed, the education of many senior managers actually trains them to consider what will happen if they do nothing, as a part of the risk management process.[4]

In fact, sooner or later, something adverse, and no one can actually predict precisely what, is *going* to happen; that is inevitable, and we just don't know what or when! When an adverse event *does* occur, how well the local hospital is able to respond to the event, recover, and continue to provide for the needs of the community will become a central point of discussion regarding the facility's reputation for years to come. As such, the event will either play a huge role in garnering both community support and fundraising efforts or these key issues will be damaged because of it.

Such results are not impossible; consider the example of a local hospital literally destroyed by a direct tornado strike, which was able to set up and operate a temporary full-service emergency room in improvised facilities within about two hours, while the facility itself was still being evacuated, and a temporary hospital, in modular facilities, within a week.[5] That hospital will be forever held dear in the minds of local residents and will be the target of both direct donations and fund-raising efforts for years to come! The challenge is for the Emergency Manager to convince the CEO and senior management that such large-scale resources, and large-scale integration and cooperation with facilities which are viewed as competitors, are both worthwhile and appropriate.

Lack of Coordination

The lack of coordination between healthcare facilities during a crisis is typically either the result of communications failures or of a fundamental disconnect in information and work direction caused by differing Command and Control systems.[6] To illustrate, if in one hospital a variant of the incident management system model is in place, but in the neighboring hospital, the crisis is run by the vice-president/nursing and a group of nursing unit administrators, how are these two groups going to figure out the lines of communications and the process flow required to make any type of real coordination even feasible? Without a common Command and Control model, formal coordination remains difficult, at best.

While coordination between healthcare facilities is desirable, the ability of a healthcare facility to coordinate their activities with those of the emergency services and of the community at large is also every bit as important. The time to begin to establish robust communications between all of the agencies involved is not during a major incident. Such discussions should begin months or even years in advance. The best way to accomplish this is through regionally coordinated training with common models and through ongoing interagency dialog resulting from regular interagency planning meetings and discussions.[7]

Figure 3.1 Healthcare Emergency Managers activate a hospital's Emergency Management Plan

The incident command system has humble beginnings, as a model for the coordination of fire service activities, across a fireground. The incident management/incident command systems, in their various iterations including both HICS and HECCS, have found their way into broad usage across a range of vastly different service providers, specifically because they permit highly effective coordination between organizations which may not even have a day-to-day dialog.[8] Truthfully, while many practitioners may have specific model preferences, it doesn't truly matter which Command and Control model is used, as long as it is used consistently and by all involved in the incident.

Interfacility Communications

Communications failures are one of the greatest single challenges to safety in contemporary hospitals, even on a day-to-day basis. The Joint Commission lists "Communications Failures" as a leading root cause of adverse events occurring in the hospitals which it serves, over a period of years.[9] Not all communication is technology based, but in a disaster situation in which multiple hospitals and other healthcare providers are attempting to share critical information while lacking interoperable communications networks or communications protocols, the potential for disastrous errors is greatly increased.

With respect to communications failures, these are most often the result of a failure to have formal emergency communications arrangements in place, in advance of any disaster event. That being said, communications failure is almost always a risk factor in disasters of all types.[10] In many cases, it becomes a matter of not understanding the limitations of various communications technologies, not having robust backup systems in place, or even simply not agreeing in advance on how facilities will contact each other during any crisis.

To illustrate, if the organizations elect to use telephones, have they considered what might occur if the telephone network fails or is overwhelmed? The telephone networks in most developed countries can only accommodate the simultaneous use of about 20 percent of the telephones on the network, and in developing countries, this capacity is often much lower. If the facilities are contemplating simply telephoning one another, those calls will go through a switchboard, generally at both ends of the call. If the switchboard is overwhelmed at either end of the call, communications will fail.

If the facilities are using Voice Over Internet Protocol (VoIP) telephony, they are dependent upon the continued functioning of their Internet Service Provider to maintain communications.[11] Neither cellular (mobile) or the so-called "smart" phones provide a reasonable alternative, since both are entirely dependent upon the main telephone network. Choices can be made, along with robust backup strategies, but they need to be agreed upon in advance. Without effective communications, there can be no effective coordination. The challenge is to make appropriate choices, to agree upon their use, to develop backup systems, and to test all of these in advance.

Credentialing of Staff

The process of allowing new professional staff to work inside your facility is not a simple one. Contrary to public belief, a given hospital cannot simply permit an unknown physician or nurse to arrive at the facility and begin treating patients, even during a disaster! There are huge potential liability issues which may be involved. When a new physician or nurse, or a similar professional, applies to join the staff of a given healthcare facility, a complex and detailed background check always occurs.[12] Did this person actually graduate from a recognized medical/nursing school? Have they passed state/provincial licensing examinations? Do they actually have the specialty training that they claim to have? Have references been discussed with previous employers? Have there been any incidents of professional misconduct or professional discipline by their licensing body? If they have worked in another jurisdiction, has that jurisdiction also been checked? Has a police background check been conducted? This may seem somewhat excessive, but it is absolutely necessary, in order to protect the patients, other staff members, and the hospital from fraudulent, incompetent, or undesirable practitioners.[13]

This may sound extreme, but in fact, in most jurisdictions, the processes described occur every time that a new member of the professional staff is employed, or, in the case of physicians, joins the staff as a contractor. This process is absolutely central to the ability of the facility to demonstrate due diligence, should anything ever go wrong, and they find themselves in litigation. It is also a central condition to most liability and medical malpractice insurance policies, which healthcare facilities are often required by law to have in place.

Such comprehensive background checks can take two or more weeks to complete. As a result, they cannot take place during the time of

Hospital credentialing process

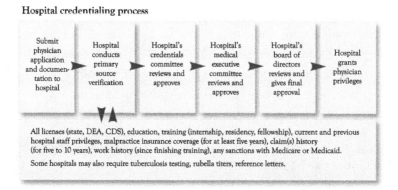

Figure 3.2 Credentialing is a complex and detailed task, but an essential one. It cannot occur effectively in the middle of a crisis response

occurrence of a disaster. This can often pose a major barrier to the sharing of staff by multiple facilities during a crisis. If a nurse, for example, is employed at two hospitals, each has completed their own background credentialing process, and so, that one particular nurse may work in either facility, but apart from that, it is nearly impossible for one hospital to simply loan nurses or physicians to another hospital, even during a crisis. For such arrangements to be effective, they would require extensive advance discussion, formal agreements, and probably an advance process of the cross-credentialing of each facility's staff by each of the other facilities involved in the agreement.

Exploring Solutions

In truth, the failures of healthcare systems to successfully perform advance integration of their respective emergency response systems are more common than most would wish to believe. Such failure is typically the directly result of healthcare facilities failing to place priorities on emergency preparedness activities and on their normal practice of viewing other healthcare facilities as potential competitors, and, as a result, the development and creation of those preparedness activities which do occur within carefully guarded silos. In some cases, there appears to be an attitude that the disclosure of potential vulnerabilities to a competitor places the facility at a competitive disadvantage.

In fact, the full and frank sharing of such information, along with collaboration to address those vulnerabilities, tends to make a facility less, rather than more, vulnerable to the effects of an adverse event. Through the sharing of knowledge and through collaboration with colleagues at other facilities, the healthcare-based Emergency Manager can provide the facility with leadership in integrating preparedness activities and can become a force for change within each facility.

Common Operating Systems

The management of emergencies is primarily about four issues: Command and Control, communications, coordination of resources, and supply chains. These four issues do not change significantly inside of a healthcare facility, and these issues will often form some of the potential barriers to successful coordination between healthcare facilities. They are, therefore, a good starting point from which the Emergency Manager, along with colleagues at other facilities, may begin to overcome those barriers to cooperation and coordination, which often exist between the various healthcare facilities in the same region.

Command and Control Models

The first of these, Command and Control, is often the easiest to overcome; if all facilities are using the same Command and Control model, usually a variant of the incident management system, then the model itself can assist with coordination. Command and Control models will be discussed in considerable detail elsewhere in this series; however, for now, it is sufficient to say that when all facilities use the same Command and Control model, they will populate the same Key Roles (e.g., logistics), within each Hospital Command Center and conduct their business in more or less the same manner. The potential exists for those Key Roles to become highly effective points of information exchange and coordination, by simply engaging in regular dialog with each other at the Key Role level.[14] If there are four hospitals in a community which is responding to a disaster, why shouldn't the public information leads from all four Hospital Command Centers conduct a cooperative and coordinated media plan, with the media and the public receiving exactly the same information, regardless of which source it came from? Examples of this same level of coordination are possible between those in virtually any of the Key Roles.

Communications

With respect to communications, the issue is not so much differences in technology as an agreement to communicate specific information with other healthcare stakeholders on a regular basis. This can occur using any variety of technology from telephones to digital messaging; the key is for all to agree to use the same system. As but one example, in more than one hospital, the author has encountered the use of BlackBerry devices to achieve and coordinate all messaging, both internal and external. These devices were selected because of their tremendous flexibility, including the storage of their plan, Job Action Sheets, and all telephone number lists on each individual device, thereby ensuring that any manager with a device could run the entire incident.[15]

The use of the Facebook Messenger, WhatsApp, or Zoom software permits teleconferencing and even videoconferencing in a reasonably secure environment. The ability to conference multiple devices permitted virtual "meetings" and the ready exchange of information, and this particular system, as of this writing, has as high a level of security as any mobile device-based system in the world. Such devices can also be conferenced with similar devices in other hospitals, in order to enhance communications and to make communications networks more resilient.

High technology is not always the easiest solution. Occasionally, simple solutions just work better! In Toronto, Canada, all of the hospitals and some other healthcare stakeholders (e.g., Public Health) in the region are equipped with a UHF trunking radio, operating on a network belonging to Toronto Paramedic Service, which permits all of the healthcare stakeholders to communicate among them on a private channel during a crisis. Each radio is installed, not, as one might expect, in the emergency department, but in the room designated as the Hospital Command Center for each facility. It is connected to the facility's emergency power system, and a full-scale network test occurs once each month. The intent is to provide local healthcare stakeholders with a sound method of both exchanging information and coordinating activities, even during a regionwide electrical power failure!

In many facilities, emergency backup communications can be provided by local amateur radio operators. This is an often-overlooked community resource, and the members of organizations, such as the Amateur Radio Emergency Service (ARES), community-minded volunteers, are often willing to come into a hospital and set up robust backup emergency communications during a crisis. This can permit hospitals to maintain linkages with other healthcare providers, emergency services, and the municipal Emergency Operations Center. These amateurs can provide, at a minimum, two-way voice communication, but many can also move data, and some, even video. Such arrangements require advance negotiation, and while the volunteer will typically bring the radio equipment, the facility will have to preinstall emergency power connections and a suitable antenna.

Figure 3.3 Although older technology, radio amateurs can provide an immensely useful service to hospitals, particularly during a crisis or an exercise

In many facilities and regions, the development of a simple system of "back channel" telephone numbers operates just as effectively. Each facility or organization has a designated telephone number, or series of telephone numbers, which are unpublished and which are not routed through the facility switchboards. Such telephone numbers have the "Caller ID" feature blocked, and the actual telephone numbers are closely guarded by all involved. In this manner, even when switchboards are overwhelmed, it remains possible for each hospital to directly and immediately contact another Hospital Command Center, the municipal Emergency Operations Center, emergency services, and public utilities! In many circumstances, "low-tech" approaches are often more amenable to use during a crisis. Success in interfacility crisis communications actually has very little to do with the degree of technology. The key to successfully overcoming crisis communications barriers is for all agencies to agree in advance to use a single system for the sharing of information.

Resource Management

Resource coordination may be more of a challenge. In fact, the biggest challenge in this regard may simply be a matter of improving the collective understanding of precisely which resources a given facility does or does not possess. From a clinical perspective, there is often sufficient understanding for one facility to understand which services are available at another facility or, at least, they often think that they do. Local hospital networks often evolve along the lines of primary, secondary, and tertiary care facilities, with level and complexity of care available increasing at each stage, from the relatively small, local community hospital which offers basic services at the primary level, to university-affiliated teaching hospitals offering a broad range of advanced services, at the tertiary level.

This system is, however, changing in some important ways. In many communities, particularly in North America, the concept of a "general" hospital is starting to disappear, as technology and economics frequently force individual hospitals into more specialized roles.[16] To illustrate, it has been argued that in many communities, the experience of the emergency physicians in dealing with myocardial infarction (heart attack) is eroding, as paramedics begin to use more advanced diagnostics in the field, identifying patients with specific needs and by-passing the traditional stop in the emergency department, in order to transport the patient as quickly as possible to an interventional cardiologist, who can actually fix the patient's medical problem.[17] As a result, emergency physicians simply don't see very many of this type of patient anymore, unless they happen to walk in.

Similar initiatives are in place for trauma patients, burn patients, stroke patients, obstetrics patients, and pediatric patients, in many centers. Indeed, if current trends continue, the average emergency department may ultimately evolve into something of an advance-level family practice clinic. This is not so far-fetched a notion; in many parts of Europe, actual emergency departments in some hospitals are either minimal or nonexistent. In many cases, there is no recognized specialty in emergency medicine, but "emergency doctors" (often anesthesiologists or surgeons) respond on appropriate calls with the ambulance, stabilize the patient in the field, and then have them transported to the hospital as a direct admission. Increasingly, the old assumptions that "my local hospital can handle anything" have become erroneous, and it is increasingly necessary to have a clear understanding of which types of services are normally available, which types are unavailable, and which types the hospital is prepared to offer specifically during a crisis.

What might be less understood is what nonclinical resources a given hospital might have that might be accessed by another hospital during a crisis. Does one hospital have an out-patient program which has caused it to acquire passenger vans or mini-buses? Such resources are also often found in long-term care facilities, which are often ignored by hospitals for planning purposes. Does one hospital have a particular service available in-house that the other hospitals in the network do not? This might include an in-house information technology department, where other hospitals have contracted this service out. Such resources might include a standing inventory of patient care equipment, although in the age of "just-in-time" inventory control, such resources are becoming increasingly rare. Does one hospital have an in-house linen laundry system, while all of the others are dependent on a delivery system which may be affected by the current crisis? The list can go on, reaching into many facilities and many in-house departments which Emergency Managers might not normally consider. All of these somewhat obscure services are resources which might need to be shared with other facilities during a crisis, and so, the capabilities and the limitations of all must be clearly understood in advance.

Coordinated Planning

A key step to the creation of a truly integrated emergency response by a healthcare system is the development of an ability by all participating facilities within each network to begin to conduct their emergency preparedness planning in a cooperative and coordinated manner. When facilities begin to plan together, the opportunity to eliminate many of the potential barriers to success is created. Unnecessary duplication of services is created when services can be potentially shared, staff training can become standardized, and staff training and exercises may be conducted jointly; and with that standardization resulting in reduced deviation from procedure and increased elimination of errors—both key features of the Six Sigma management model. While not the primary considerations, it may well be the case that time wasted on the unnecessary duplication of services and also money wasted on the unnecessary duplication resources, as well as on both staff training and exercises, may also be saved, a key attribute of Lean for Healthcare.

Resource Sharing

The savings possible through the use of formal resource-sharing programs and arrangements should be immediately obvious; a facility which is permitted to share a resource from another facility may not need to acquire that resource for itself, or to pay the full cost of the maintenance of that resource, between uses. In some healthcare jurisdictions, particularly in the United States and Canada, there is evolution of the healthcare system from large numbers of individual hospitals operating independently, into larger corporate entities, or pseudo-governmental agencies sometimes called regional health authorities, which operate as a single corporate entity with multiple operating sites (the hospitals).

One tremendous advantage to this model is that by having a single employer of record operating multiple sites, combined with a single credentialing system and a single insurance carrier, it can become much easier to coordinate Emergency Management across multiple sites within a region. There is also a trend toward the replacement of the use of multiple individuals at various worksites spending a smaller part of each day on

Emergency Management activities, to a full-time individual or individuals, operating at a corporate level, and providing guidance and expertise to all of the operating sites. There are clear advantages to the practice of resource sharing, although the precise form will vary from one organization to the next, in terms of what has been included in such arrangements and what has not been included.

Personnel

The exchange of professional personnel between facilities has already been discussed at length in this chapter and will not be further belabored. Suffice it to say that in any system with a single corporate entity operating multiple service delivery sites as a single employer of record, the free movement of professional staff between the various operating sites as needed is a relatively simple matter. In systems with multiple hospitals and clinics within a region, operating as multiple individual employers of record, it becomes much more complex to move staff from one facility to another, even in times of need, without a considerable amount of advance discussions, signed agreements, advance cross-credentialing processes, and the approval of liability, worker's compensation, and medical malpractice insurance carriers.

Materiel and Other Resources

The voluntary sharing of some resources is not at all problematic; if such resources are readily available, one hospital may be able to freely share bed linens, food, or, in some cases, cleaning supplies. One hospital may agree to provide information technology support staff to another hospital which normally contracts out such services, in some circumstances. There are, however, limitations to what could potentially be shared, even during a crisis, without careful advance planning. To illustrate, one hospital is using intravenous solutions and supplies from one manufacturer, while the next closest hospital is using the same type of equipment from a different manufacturer. In a crisis, one hospital would be prevented from sharing its inventory of intravenous equipment with the other hospital, because the two sets of equipment are incompatible with one another.

They cannot be used together, and the staff of the receiving facility has not received training in the use of the equipment from the other facility.

The issue of most hospitals using "just-in-time" inventory management is also a major factor, as administrators pare away surplus inventory wherever they can in order to eliminate waste and save money, without much consideration of the needs generated by a disaster.[18] This problem could conceivably be overcome, either through the advance training of the staff of both facilities or through an orchestrated advance decision for both hospitals to use equipment from the same manufacturer.

There are any number of resource-sharing issues which would face similar challenges, and almost all could potentially be overcome through the use of coordinated, cooperative resource acquisition planning, conducted in advance. These include such resources as the hospital pharmacy, medical equipment management, medical electronics, and other types of medical devices, such as ventilators. There are already individuals with specific expertise in such matters in most hospitals; the Emergency Manager does not need to be able to operate the supply chain, simply to understand it, and to find potential opportunities for improvement and cooperation, conducted under the mantle of Emergency Management.

Sharing Workload

Hospitals are particularly vulnerable to unscheduled demands for service. While there is probably a public perception that the local hospital stands ready and waiting, with every resource required to cope with an emergency, this is not necessarily the case. Hospitals, and their resources, such as diagnostic equipment and operating theaters, tend to be very heavily scheduled, and while some buffers are probably in place for unscheduled events, this does not include major emergency events. Many hospitals operate on a daily basis at, or even beyond, their capacity to provide care and the impact of such events has the potential to throw even a well-ordered hospital into chaos relatively quickly. This is immediately worsened, when a single hospital bears the brunt of the patient load generated by the entire event by itself, with a need to reschedule diagnostic procedures and surgeries and to find beds for new patients, in a facility which is already full.

Fortunately, this problem does not need to create as severe an impact if local hospitals are willing to cooperate with one another. Historically, there has existed a tendency for healthcare facilities to conduct their emergency planning activities in silos; this is primarily due to the unfortunate tendency to view one another as competitors. Advance planning is required, and all of the local hospitals will need to be brought to the table. Whenever possible, the time to decide what to do should not occur in the middle of the crisis.

With such planning, it is entirely possible to arrive at an agreement as to precisely how the victims of a mass-casualty incident will be distributed, whether based upon simple numbers or upon levels of clinical acuity. It is also possible to arrive at a plan to assist "first-impact" hospitals by agreeing to receive and continue the care of some of their existing in-patients, in order to make space for disaster victims. Another essential player in this problem-solving discussion is the local EMS system; paramedics don't particularly want to overwhelm a particular facility, and if alternatives are being explored, they will generally be happy to participate; after all, they have an Emergency Plan to write, as well.

Balanced Emergency Patient Distribution

At a mass-casualty incident, the local EMS system will be primarily responsible for the assignment of a destination hospital for each patient. This function is usually performed by a transport officer, taking into consideration clinical issues which have been identified during the field triage and treatment process. The process usually also attempts to consider each hospital's treatment capabilities, local policies, and regulations, and the amount and type of transportation resources which are immediately available. Bear in mind that EMS, like the hospital, has limited resources available and must cope with not only the current crisis, but every other emergency occurring simultaneously within the community. Similarly, while the care of paramedics is usually excellent over the short term, asking them to manage patients with complex treatment requirements over an extended period is very likely to exceed their scope of practice. As a result, it may be unrealistic and inappropriate to expect that they will transport clinically acute patients over large distances without stopping at a closer hospital for stabilization of the patient.

It is also appropriate to remember that in many mass-casualty sit-uations, many of the victims are not transported to hospital by EMS; they arrive in a variety of modes of transport, often untriaged, untreated, and without any prior decontamination.[19] With those conditions in mind, and an appropriate advance agreement in place, EMS systems are generally quite willing to attempt to distribute the load as evenly as pos-sible, across several local hospitals, and that distribution may be based upon simple numbers or upon clinical acuity.

Even when this does not occur through EMS, usually because of normal transportation arrangements and protocols, it is almost certainly going to be necessary for the various facilities and agencies to arrive at a reasonable arrangement for the accessing of in-patient beds. This will normally occur through the redistribution, including the decanting, of existing in-patients, in order to make space for the influx of victims who are in more immediate need of acute care beds. This means that not only the local acute care facilities will be affected, but there will be a secondary effect as the existing in-patients are either decanted to more distant facilities or discharged to long-term care or care in the community. Arrangements will be required with the providers of all of these services, and the best time to achieve them is in advance, so that they can be incorporated into all Emergency Response Plans.

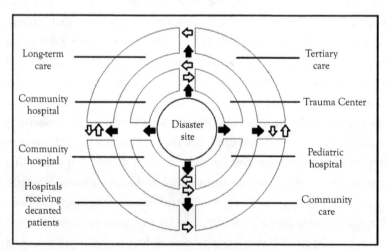

Figure 3.4 The management of any mass-casualty event is a complex process, likely to require extensive interfacility cooperation and the redistribution of patients across the entire continuum of care

Predetermined Clinical Roles

Distribution of disaster patients according to clinical issues is one potential option, but it is a complex one. In an age in which some hospitals attempt to specialize, there is an increasing, but somewhat erroneous, assumption that the specialty resource will receive all patients which fall into its area of specialization. Trauma Centers are an excellent case in point; on a daily basis it is perfectly reasonable to assume that all trauma patients will be transported to that location. However, in a mass-casualty event, it is equally likely that the local Trauma Center will very quickly exceed its treatment capacity for trauma patients, forcing community hospitals back into the "trauma business." This is a situation which can also occur for other areas of specialization, such as burns.

Instead, it may be more appropriate to classify hospitals according to both distance from the disaster event and clinical treatment capabilities. "First impact" hospitals would be those in the closest proximity to the event, thereby necessitating the shortest transport times to definitive care for those victims with the highest levels of clinical acuity. "Second impact" hospitals would be those further away, and hopefully, dealing with the lower acuity patients, and receiving higher acuity cases only when the first impact hospitals exceeded their capacity. "Predesignated" hospitals would provide specialty care, such as Trauma Centers, for as long as they were able, with their overflow being passed to the first impact hospitals. A final classification, "overflow" hospitals, would be those furthest away, and their role would be to accept redirected routine emergency patient traffic in order to permit the first impact hospitals to deal with the crisis, and also any in-patients being decanted from the first impact hospitals, or stabilized disaster patients who were being transferred for admission, to make space for victims in the first impact hospitals. With the exception of the "predesignated" hospitals, the actual role of each hospital in the network would be determined in each new event, according to its physical proximity to the disaster event.

It may be useful and appropriate to map out the entire prehospital patient distribution scheme in advance. Tools such as Value Stream Mapping and spatial data plotting could contribute substantially to this process. Such a model would require the agreement and cooperation of

EMS, all regional hospitals, and other local healthcare stakeholders. This research, planning, and approval of the required agreements would need to be completed in advance of any emergency event, with healthcare Emergency Managers likely to play an important role in both leading and guiding a representative planning group.

Receiving Decanted In-Patients

All hospitals are essentially boxes of finite size, even during a disaster! All hospitals have the potential to reach a point of patient "saturation," particularly during a disaster event. Space will eventually be required for many of the victims to be treated as in-patients, particularly after they have cleared the "bottlenecks" in the emergency department, diagnostic procedures, and surgery. The space required may involve an intensive care setting or a less clinically intense setting. The management of this problem is essentially an exercise in surge capacity, at each stage along the continuum of care. As such, it may benefit directly from a joint examination of crisis bed management, using such methodologies as Value Stream Mapping, in order to find new efficiencies in the process of patient flow. Such activities should be conducted jointly by the various facilities in the regional hospital network, using those with clinical expertise, bed management expertise, and the Emergency Manager.

There are really only two options for the management of such patients. One may stabilize these patients, and then transfer them by ambulance to a more distant facility with both space available and the ability to treat that particular patient's condition. As an alternative, one may consider the transfer of existing low-acuity in-patients. This would include those in-patients on elective admissions, those awaiting long-term care placements, or those expected to be discharged to care in the community within the next 48 hours. These patients could potentially be moved from the first impact hospitals to more distant hospitals or other venues of care, in order to create in-patient space for those victims of the disaster who require it. While admittedly complex and disruptive, the latter is generally the safer means of managing this issue, since those patients with the lowest clinical acuity and the least treatment requirements are those being transported, while those with the higher clinical acuity and treatment requirements consistently remain in the safer environment. Such bed management methodologies need to be determined in advance, and they should be the subject of both advance dialog and formal agreements between all of the facilities involved.

Methods of Fostering Integration

Healthcare facilities are unlikely to work together unless they first begin by talking together. In order to achieve the required objectives, all must be shown how cooperation is in their mutual interest, despite their normal, and somewhat outdated, positioning as competitors. The most likely keys to fostering this type of self-serving cooperation would include minimizing business disruptions and the reduction of costs, as well as the elimination of waste and the elimination of errors. All of these issues are already generally fairly high on the "radar" of most healthcare Chief Executive Officers.

The introduction of mainstream business management techniques, such as Lean for Healthcare and Six Sigma, are likely to add substantially to the interest of senior managers in such an initiative, and the techniques of Project Management are likely to contribute to the success of related projects. Committee work, although time-consuming, is clearly necessary in order to build an atmosphere of cooperation and consensus, because people are much more likely to cooperate with those with whom they already enjoy a relationship. Indeed, it may be possible for the Emergency Managers of the various facilities to harness some of that traditional competitive attitude and energy in order to move related projects along the path to completion and implementation more quickly and efficiently.

The development of a regional healthcare Emergency Preparedness Committee is generally a good place at which to begin. Under the guidance of a working group consisting of the facilities' own Emergency Managers, a preparedness framework can be developed, in which various major issues can be discussed. These may include, but are not limited to, a comprehensive HIRA for the regional healthcare network, a common Command and Control model, integrated communications, mutual support agreements, jointly conducted in-service education and emergency exercises, and negotiated agreements regarding patient distribution and specific facility roles during a disaster.

Don't forget to include long-term care in the discussion; their plans are likely to affect acute care facilities, and they can provide a valuable resource for receiving decanted patients, during an emergency. As a first step, consider having all of the healthcare agencies in the region share a copy of their own Emergency Plan with one another; these can greatly improve understanding and can provide an invaluable resource to each Hospital Command Center, during a large-scale crisis. From the perspective of the Emergency Manager, all of this can often be conducted under the banner of being able to demonstrate community partnerships as a part of the accreditation process.

Conclusion

In many parts of the world, healthcare providers tend to view each other as competitors. Depending on the type of healthcare system, this may take the form of good-natured competitiveness or it can be a "no nonsense" serious challenge for market share by two or more large business entities. In either case, in a disaster response, such challenges must be set aside, in order to permit a coordinated and cooperative response aimed at benefiting the greatest number of injured victims. The Emergency Manager is uniquely situated within the healthcare facility to overcome those barriers discreetly and quietly to collaboration, to become a force for change within their own facility, and to put technologies, lines of communication, resources, and procedures into place which have the potential to permit highly effective coordination during times of crisis, between facilities which view themselves as competitors on a daily basis. Working together can be made a "win–win" situation for healthcare facilities and will undoubtedly benefit the victims of any disaster.

Student Projects

Student Project #1

Select a single hospital as the subject hospital and conduct an inventory of available onsite clinical and physical plant maintenance resources. Identify any resource-sharing arrangements with other hospitals which are already in place. Identify all other hospitals which are located within a 30-minute drive of the subject hospital, and identify any clinical (e.g., intensive care unit) or physical plant maintenance (e.g., IT department) resources which are not normally available in the subject hospital, which might be required during any emergency event. Draft a plan for disaster cooperation between all of the hospitals in question. Be sure to identify potential barriers to cooperation and to propose potential solutions to these problems. Be sure to cite and reference as required, in order to demonstrate that sufficient appropriate research has occurred.

Student Project #2

Create a final draft of a formal mutual assistance agreement, to be entered into between three acute care hospitals and two long-term care facilities operating within a single county, within an identified jurisdiction, such as a state or a province. Be sure to include specific information on activation, Command and Control, interfacility communications, sharing of resources, resolution of disputes, and procedures for standing down. Ensure that all aspects of the mutual assistance agreement are in full compliance with all relevant Emergency Management and healthcare legislation in the jurisdiction selected. Be sure to cite and reference as required, in order to demonstrate that sufficient appropriate research has occurred.

Test Your Knowledge

Take your time. Read each question carefully and select the *most correct* answer for each. The correct answers appear at the end of the section. If you score less than 80 percent (8 correct answers) you should reread this chapter.

1. Some emergency response issues which create substantial barriers to coordinating the responses of multiple healthcare facilities include:

   (a) Different Command and Control systems
   (b) Lack of interoperable communications
   (c) Conflicting in-house policies
   (d) All of the above

2. Issues which provide barriers to the free movement of professional staff from one hospital to another include insurance requirements and:

(a) Credentialing of staff
(b) Legislative barriers
(c) Policy barriers
(d) Both (b) and (c)

3. Issues which can potentially create unforeseen problems when hospitals attempt to cooperate during a crisis are that they frequently:

(a) View each other as competitors
(b) Have unrealistic expectations of each other
(c) Lack a complete understanding of each other's available resources
(d) All of the above

4. Regionwide cooperation by those Emergency Managers working with healthcare facilities can provide:

(a) Effective joint exercises and training
(b) Reduced operating costs
(c) A good public image
(d) All of the above

5. An advantage of using a Command and Control model within a group of healthcare facilities, such as the incident management system, is that it can:

(a) Provide a common response framework
(b) Provide effective points of interfacility information sharing
(c) Provide effective points of resource coordination
(d) All of the above

6. Balanced distribution of patients from a mass-casualty incident can ensure that patients obtain improved times to treatment and:

(a) Individual hospitals are less overwhelmed and can provide better care
(b) Transport times for patients improve

(c) Patients with serious injuries are sent to the most advanced hospitals

(d) All of the above

7. An unfortunate reality of Trauma Centers is that they have finite capacities, and as soon as those capacities are exceeded:

(a) More staff will be called in to work in improvised spaces

(b) Other surrounding hospitals will have to begin treating trauma patients

(c) Patients will need to be transported to more distant Trauma Centers

(d) Both (a) and (c)

8. An unfortunate reality of Emergency Management in healthcare is that every time a healthcare facility must be evacuated, or must decant stable in-patients in order to receive disaster patients, their actions may generate:

(a) Increases in local demand for service

(b) Staffing shortages

(c) A "de facto" mass-casualty incident for surrounding facilities

(d) Both (a) and (b)

9. Regional Healthcare Emergency Preparedness Committees, composed of the Emergency Managers from all healthcare facilities in a given region, may result in:

(a) Improved interfacility coordination during a crisis

(b) Improved understanding of each facility's capabilities and limitations

(c) Improved standardization of Emergency Response Plans

(d) All of the above

10. An essential requirement of any mutual assistance agreement negotiated between various types of healthcare facilities is that the agreement must:

(a) Comply with all relevant local laws and regulations

(b) Be signed by each facility's Chief Executive Officer

(c) Be approved by local government

(d) All of the above

Answers

1. (d)   2. (a)   3. (d)   4. (a)   5. (d)
6. (a)   7. (b)   8. (c)   9. (d)   10. (a)

Additional Reading

The author recommends the following exceptionally good titles as supplemental readings, which will help to enhance the student's knowledge of those topics covered in this chapter:

Abkowitz, M. Fall 2008. *Lessons Learned the Hard Way: What Disasters Can Teach Us About Planning, Communication, and Luck.* Vanderbilt Magazine, Vanderbilt University. www.vanderbilt.edu/magazines/vanderbilt-magazine/2008/10/lessons-learned-the-hard-way/ (accessed online February 04, 2014).

CNA. 2009. *Medical Staff Credentialing: Eight Strategies for Safer Physician and Provider Privileging.* CNA, Chicago: Vantage Point magazine, 09:3. (accessed online February 04, 2014).

Donahue, A.K. and R.V. Tuohy. July 2006. "Lessons We Don't Learn: A Study of the Lessons of Disasters, Why We Repeat Them, and How We Can Learn Them." *Journal of the Naval Postgraduate School Center for Homeland Defence and Security,* .pdf document. www.hsaj.org/?fullarticle=2.2.4 (accessed online February 04, 2014).

FEMA. 2004. *NIMS and the Incident Command System: A Position Paper.* Washington: US Federal Emergency Management Agency. www.fema.gov/txt/nims/nims_ics_position_paper.txt (accessed online February 04, 2014).

Risk and Compromise Tool. 2012. On-Pace, Ohio State University webpage. http://onpace.osu.edu/posts/documents/Risk%20and%20Compromise%20Tool.pdf (accessed online February 04, 2014).

CHAPTER 4

An Emergency Management for Healthcare Glossary

As in most specialized fields, there exists, within the practice of Emergency Management for healthcare and Emergency Management in general, a jargon of sorts, which has evolved among users, over a period of time. This jargon set flows from a variety of similar sources, although these have historically been not well connected. These include firefighting, law enforcement, mainstream Emergency Management, healthcare clinical practice and administration, and general business management. These will be encountered and expected in most aspects of professional practice, so the student would do well to learn these and to incorporate them into the various documents and other forms of communication which will be expected of them.

Glossary of Terms

Accreditation: A structured, peer-based review of the quality of operations and services provided by a given healthcare organization. Such reviews are intended to be comprehensive, consistent, objective, and transparent, and most hospitals and other healthcare organizations regard them as an essential indicator of quality. Such reviews typically operate on a three- to four-year cycle and are conducted by a number of different organizations around the world.

Accreditation Canada: A Canadian-based healthcare accreditation organization, which also operates internationally.

Active Monitoring Status: A given infectious disease has been identified within the community, or nearby, requiring the healthcare facility to monitor the situation closely and begin preparations for the reception and treatment of any potential cases which may arrive. Such information is normally found on a national/federal government health department website or on a state/provincial government health department website.

After Action Report: A final report summarizing actions, experiences, occurrences, and recommendations, written by the Incident Manager or the Emergency Manager, following an actual emergency event. They are used to share experiences and "lessons learned." Such documents are usually directed to senior management staff and are typically held indefinitely.

After Exercise Report: A final report summarizing actions, experiences, occurrences, and recommendations, written by the Incident Manager or the Emergency Manager, following an emergency exercise of any type. They are used to share experiences and "lessons learned." They may also be used to demonstrate the presence of an emergency preparedness program during institutional accreditation processes. Such documents are usually directed to senior management staff and are typically held indefinitely.

Airborne Organism: Used to describe a pathogen which is carried freely on the air, and usually absorbed by means of inhalation.

Alert Status: A given infectious disease outbreak has been identified somewhere in the world but is not yet present in the institution or its immediate community. Monitoring of information is typically less intense and occurs through the regular review of such tools as the World Health Organization website.

"All-Hazards": An older approach to the practice of Emergency Management, in which it is accepted that it is impossible to prepare for each individual event, and so attempts to generate a generic "general preparedness" level, capable of coping at a reasonable level with any type of event which may occur. This approach has largely been replaced by risk-based approaches to preparedness and planning.

Amateur Radio: A group of hobbyists, present in many countries, whose interest is in electronic broadcast communications of all types. Originally only Morse Code and two-way voice transmission, such hobbyists now focus on voice, data, and, in some cases, even television. Such hobbyists pride themselves on being able to communicate at great distances, and in their ability to maintain and repair their own equipment. There are some groups of amateurs whose primary focus is emergency communications support to various types of agencies, including hospitals, in times of crisis. Such organizations include the Amateur Radio Emergency Service (Canada), Radio Amateur Civil Emergency Service (United States), RAYNET (United Kingdom), Amateur Radio Emergency Communications (New Zealand), and Wireless Institute Civil Emergency Network (Australia).

Applied Research: Refers to the scientific study and research which is used to solve practical problems. Applied research is used to solve everyday problems, treat illnesses, and develop innovative technologies. This type of research is often used in the fields of psychology, social sciences, and medicine.

Australian Emergency Manual Series: A comprehensive collection of booklets and small books, providing detailed instructions dealing with a broad range of disaster-related activities and topics. The collection is published by Emergency Management Australia.

Barrier Precautions: Those strategies which are intended to place a physical barrier between the infected patient and others, in order to prevent the movement of the disease organism from one host to another. These include physical isolation, such as holding the infected patient(s) in pre-designated rooms, ideally with a specially designed system of closed circulation and filtration of air. These measures also include articles of clothing, often disposable, which place a barrier between an infectious patient and the means of absorption of the organism. These might include various categories of face masks, eye protection, gloves, and protective clothing, in some cases, fully encapsulated suits and respirators. Also included is the practice of regular, meticulous, consistent handwashing, ideally with antiseptic soap and/or alcohol gel, each time a staff member enters or leaves the room. Finally, these measures include the safe disposal of any waste generated by the care of the patient.

Beaufort Wind Speed Scale: A method of describing and classifying in-line winds, according to wind speed, and to observable characteristics in the environment resulting from the actions of those winds.

Bed Clearance Team: A multidisciplinary team which is tasked with the rapid but organized discharge of suitable existing in-patients, in order to make space available for new patients generated by some external event.

Blood/Bodily Fluid Borne: As the name suggests, the pathogen moves from one host to another through direct exposure to blood, saliva, urine, feces, semen, or other bodily secretions.

Broadcast Radio: The transmission of information, news, music, and so on, from a local source to receivers in homes and vehicles. Increasingly referred to as "terrestrial" radio, in order to distinguish it from the increasingly (at least in North America) popular satellite radio systems. Does not refer to two-way radio communications, which are treated separately.

Business Continuity Planning: A separate and distinct discipline from Emergency Management, focused on the provision of similar services to private industry and geared toward the protection and resilience of business resources and interests, and on continuity of business operations, both locally and on a global scale. This process espouses many of the same principles and objectives as Emergency Management but maintains separate training and certifications. Many of the best Emergency Managers are cross-trained and cross-certified in both disciplines.

Business Cycle: A series of regularly scheduled, minuted meetings in the Hospital/Healthcare Command Center, in which the members of the Incident Management Team meet with the Incident Manager for the purpose of receiving updated information and work direction, and reporting both progress and problems in the resolution of a given emergency situation. The length and timing of the business cycle meetings is variable and is determined by the Incident Manager.

Canadian Standards Association: A well-known and respected Canadian organization, operating since 1919, which creates standards covering a broad range of topics and which tests products and services for compliance with those standards.

CASE Team: (acr.) Clinical Acuity Special Needs Evacuation Team. A multidisciplinary team tasked with the safe evacuation of those patients with the highest clinical acuity and/or lowest mobility from a healthcare facility.

Choropleth: A symbol or marked and bounded area on a map, denoting the relative distribution of some resource or property (e.g., population).

Civil Defense: The forerunner of modern Emergency Management. During the period from 1939 to 1970, focused primarily, but not exclusively, on protection of the public from the effects of World War II and, subsequently, the Cold War nuclear threat.

Command Staff: An incident management system term, used to describe those Key Role positions which directly support the Incident Manager, specifically the liaison coordinator, the Public Information Coordinator, and the safety coordinator.

Contact Tracing: A process whereby the movements of an infected individual are tracked, usually over the incubation period of the disease, in order to identify, monitor, and treat all other individuals with whom the patient has had contact. Usually performed by the infection control professional or the local health department.

Debriefing: The systematic gathering of information, including facts, problems encountered, opinions, and suggestions for improvement, following the conclusion of an exercise or a real disaster event. Debriefing may be immediate and verbal ("hot wash") or more formal and questionnaire based.

Decanting: The systematic and safe removal (transfer/discharge) by a hospital of clinically appropriate patients in order to create sufficient treatment space for the new victims of a major incident.

Declaration of Emergency: A process by which, in most jurisdictions, governments signal to upper levels of government that they have exceeded their available resources in responding to a given emergency, and, in essence, inviting a flow of assistance from upper levels of government. This may be monetary assistance or may involve actual resources, such as military assistance.

Decontamination Area: A designated area outside of the facility, prior to triage and treatment areas, in which any patients who may have been exposed to chemicals or other hazardous materials are cleaned and decontaminated by specially trained staff as a safety measure, prior to commencing assessment and treatment. This measure may be necessary in order to protect staff and other patients.

DFSS: Design for Six Sigma.

Discharge Holding Center/Lounge: A designated site at which former in-patients are held and cared for until the discharge process is concluded, and transportation occurs. This is intended to expedite the availability of acute care beds and patient flow within the healthcare facility.

DMADV: Define, Measure, Analyze, Design/Deploy, Verify. A Six Sigma term for the process used for the creation of a new system of any type.

DMAIC: Define, Measure, Analyze, Improve, Control. A Six Sigma term for the process used for the modification and improvement of an existing system of any type.

Droplet Borne: In this case, the pathogen is introduced into the environment on miniscule droplets of water, usually by coughing. A second individual may inhale these droplets, transmitting the disease. These droplets can remain suspended in the air for short periods of time, but then fall onto surfaces where contact transmission also becomes possible, as secondary individuals without barriers touch contaminated surfaces, and then themselves, often their eyes, completing the chain of transmission.

Due Diligence: The care which an "average, reasonable" person or organization exercises in order to ensure that all potential contingencies have been considered and that no harm will come to any person or organization, resulting from the actions of the primary organization.

Emergency Codes: A series of predesignated code words, often colors, each for a specific type of event, often used on the overhead paging systems in healthcare organizations to discreetly inform staff that some type of emergency situation is currently in progress without alarming patients or visitors. These systems are also used to structure the planning of responses to specific types of events, often providing staff with templated step-by-step instructions for what to do in each specific circumstance. Such codes vary tremendously between various healthcare systems, with no system or individual code being truly universal.

Emergency Management: The activities undertaken by a community or an organization, in order to ensure the ability to continue operations during various types of crises, both internal and external. The practice focuses on four key features of management, specifically, preparedness, response, recovery, and mitigation. This process has its origins in the Civil Defense of the Cold War era, and indeed is still called Civil Defense or Civil Protection in some countries.

Emergency Manager: The individual(s) within a community or an organization primarily responsible for the practice of Emergency Management. The role of the Emergency Manager is increasingly being professionalized, and while practitioners were once either ex-military or emergency services staff, they are increasingly being trained in university degree programs, with designated certifications of competency, such as the Certified Emergency Manager designation in use by the International Association of Emergency Managers.

Emergency Medical Service (EMS): Paramedics and ambulances. Known in the United Kingdom primarily as Ambulance Service, and increasingly, elsewhere, as Paramedic Service.

Emergency Preparedness Committee: A group of middle and senior-level managers within a healthcare facility, tasked with the development and oversight of both the Emergency Response Plan and an emergency preparedness program for the organization. These individuals usually function under the guidance of the Emergency Manager and are intended to provide ongoing support to whomever occupies that role in the organization.

Emergency Radio: Two-way radio communications between the various elements of the emergency services, including police, fire, EMS, and their dispatchers and municipal Emergency Operations Centers. In some communities, this system has been expanded to include access to hospitals and to other municipal departments and other stakeholders, such as public utilities.

Enhanced Fujita Scale: A model for the ranking of the size and severity of tornadoes, primarily according to wind speed.

EOC: Emergency Operations Center. A designated location in which the leaders of the community will gather to coordinate the response to a disaster, in support of the field command.

Epidemic: The occurrence of a given infectious disease at a rate which is greater than would normally be expected. It may be in a single or in multiple locations.

Evacuation—Full: The safe, systematic, and complete removal of all patients/residents, staff, and visitors from a healthcare facility of any type during an emergency event. Evacuation may be characterized as "controlled," as with a utility failure, or as "flight-to-safety," as with an ongoing structure fire.

Evacuation—Horizontal: The safe, systematic, and complete relocation of all patients/residents, staff, and visitors from a healthcare facility of any type during an emergency event. Such relocation is on the same floor as the point of origin, but to a point of safety, typically beyond two fire doors. Horizontal evacuation may be to a staging area and may be a stage or component of a full evacuation.

Evacuation—Vertical: The safe, systematic, and complete relocation of all patients/residents, staff, and visitors from a healthcare facility of any type during an emergency event. Such relocation is from the point of origin to a safer location on a lower level of the same building, but not outside of the building. Vertical evacuation is often a stage or component of a full evacuation.

Evacuation Holding Area: A designated, exit-level location where in-patients who have been evacuated from other areas of the facility are held, pending transportation away from the affected facility.

Evacuation Route: A predesignated route (often a staircase) by which the in-patients and staff from a given care location will travel in order to achieve safe egress from the facility. Such routes are intended to eliminate congestion and make evacuation swift and orderly. Secondary routes are often preidentified for use in case the emergency event denies the use of the primary route.

Evacuation Staging Area: A predesignated safe location on or near the home unit, often immediately adjacent to the evacuation route, at which patients and staff are held until the order for a full evacuation is received. See also Evacuation—Horizontal.

Event Log: A permanent chronological record of all events, occurrences, information received, discussions, decisions, and orders given in a Hospital/Healthcare Command Center during an emergency event. The Event Log is the responsibility of the Incident Manager, but its completion is normally delegated to a Scribe. Because of the duty of completion and the fact that the Event Log is completed in real time during the incident, it is considered to be a reliable source of information and may be legally admissible into evidence in a court or public inquiry in many legal jurisdictions.

Exercises—Case Study: The researched, factual, and detailed presentation to the staff (usually management staff) of a healthcare facility of an event which has occurred in some other healthcare facility, along with a structured debriefing, aimed at identifying potential lessons to be learned or to identify similar situations, should a similar event occur in the facility receiving the presentation. Excellent tool for the identification of unresolved issues within the organization.

Exercises—Full Scale: The integrated full testing of all components of a facility's ability to respond to a given type of emergency, including debriefing. Many such tests include simulated patients and may include both staff recall and simulated treatment. The most comprehensive form of testing, but also the most expensive and disruptive.

Exercises—Functional: The isolated testing of a single, discreet element of a given facility's ability to respond to an emergency situation, along with a postevent debriefing of participants and observers. Examples of such an exercise would include, but would not be limited to, testing of telephone fan-out lists, assembly of the Hospital Command Center, or the decontamination or triage of incoming patients. Excellent for the testing and review of rarely used but necessary procedures.

Exercises—Tabletop: Conducted around a map or a floor plan, in many cases. Team of participants is presented with detailed information regarding an emergency, along with timed "inputs" of information, and are expected to respond to and deal with the emergency as a group. The group then debriefs. Excellent for experimental problem solving in a safe environment.

Family Information Center: A designated locale within the healthcare facility where family members of patients can wait in peace and privacy to receive information on loved ones who are being treated during the disaster.

Finance/Accountability Chief: In the incident management system, the role which is responsible for the approval and tracking of all ongoing expenditures related to the emergency response. Reports to the Incident Manager. A member of the control group.

Flight-to-Safety: Rapid removal from an area of imminent threat, such as a fire. While clinical considerations remain important, the first priority is the immediate movement of the patient to a safe location.

"Freelancing": A term used in some Emergency Management circles to describe a process where the individual simply begins to do whatever they think best to respond to a crisis situation, rather than following the instructions provided. This may be due to the inability to find the instructions in the Emergency Response Plan or because the instructions are either confusing or contradictory and confusing.

Frequency: How often a given disaster event actually occurs within a defined area. Sometimes also referred to as a "return rate." One of the two factors considered and ranked in a HIRA.

Gantt Chart: A type of bar chart, used for the creation of a project schedule. Such charts are often broken down into individual steps or components of a project, in order to identify their relationships, order of occurrence, ability to be conducted concurrently or consecutively, and their criticality (critical path) to the completion of a project. A major Project Management tool.

Hazard: An event which poses a threat to life, health, or property. Most hazards are typically dormant, with occurrence considered as a theoretical possibility. In Emergency Management, hazards may be described according to their origins, as natural, technological, human caused (accidental), and human caused (deliberate).

Hazard Profile: A document generated by the Emergency Manager as a part of the Hazard Identification and Risk Assessment (HIRA) process. It describes the event in terms of both frequency of occurrence and potential magnitude of occurrence. Potential locations for occurrence are also identified. Such documents are research based and often identify specific past examples of similar events, identifying specific potential risk exposures and root causes of occurrence. One such document is created for each type of hazard identified.

Hazmat: A standardized abbreviation of the term "hazardous materials," sometimes referred to as "dangerous goods." The specific term is usually coined to describe an incident in which an accidental release of some type of hazardous material has occurred, requiring an emergency response. The term is also used collectively to describe vehicles, equipment, and staff (e.g., "hazmat team") used in the response to a hazardous materials release.

HECCS: The Healthcare Emergency Command and Control System. A Command and Control model based upon both the incident command system and incident management system, with some modifications to address those specific requirements of a healthcare organization which are not adequately addressed by the original models. The system is capable of full integration and some interoperation (staff interchange is not possible) with both ICS and IMS, using the same Key Roles as points of coordination. This model was introduced in 2012 by the Ontario (Canada) Hospital Association and is recommended for use in its member hospitals and agencies.

HICS: The Hospital Incident Command System. A Command and Control model used by over 5,800 hospitals in the United States. The model has its origins in the Hospital Emergency Incident Command System (HEICS), originally developed in California, and replaced in the late 1980s. It is fully interoperable with the mainstream incident command and incident management systems, but better addresses the specific needs of the healthcare setting in disaster response.

HIRA: Hazard Identification and Risk Assessment. A research-based process in which potential hazard exposures to the facility or the community are identified, examined, and characterized with respect to both frequency of occurrence and potential magnitude of impact. Each of these characteristics is then ranked, and the resulting rankings provide priorities for most other types of Emergency Management-related activities.

Hospital Command Center: A designated location within a hospital or healthcare facility which the coordinates the organization's response to any type of emergency. In healthcare, most such facilities are not purpose-built, but consist of the adaptation of spaces used on a daily basis for other purposes. In ideal circumstances, both primary and backup locations will be identified.

Human-Caused Hazard: A hazard which results directly from human activity, as opposed to the failure of a mechanical system. Such events may be classified as accidental or deliberate (e.g., terrorism).

Incident Action Plan: A formal plan, created by the Incident Manager, for the successful resolution of an emergency incident. These plans set objectives and work assignments, maintaining focus on the response to the crisis, and will often drive the business cycle. Such plans often use elements of Project Management, treating the emergency incident much like a project.

Incident Command System (ICS): A Command and Control model with its origins in the U.S. fire services in the 1970s. It has since become an international standard for fireground management and has been accepted for use by other emergency services.

Incident Management System (IMS): A Command and Control model which evolved from ICS in the 1980s. The model is less militaristic and often less rigid in its application. This model has been accepted by a broad range of emergency services and other community services and, to some extent, by the healthcare sector.

Incident Manager: The individual in overall charge of the response to the incident. The chief strategist, appointing and/or confirming all other IMS Key Roles, developing the incident action plan, assigning all work, setting the business cycle, and running business cycle meetings. Sometimes referred to as the Incident Commander (ICS) or the Incident Controller (New Zealand) or the Gold Commander (United Kingdom).

Index Patient/Case: The first infectious patient brought to the attention of the epidemiologist.

Infection Control Professional (ICP): A medical professional, most commonly a registered nurse, who is specially trained and employed full time by a healthcare facility in order to monitor, track, and prevent transmission of and recommend control measures for infectious diseases and potentially dangerous microorganisms.

International Association of Emergency Managers (IAEM): A professional organization which supports the training and certification of Emergency Managers, based in the United States, but operating worldwide. The organization operates a formal certification process, leading to professional designation as a Certified Emergency Manager (CEM) or Associate Emergency Manager (AEM).

ISO: International Organization for Standardization. A widely respected organization which creates specific standards covering a broad range of topics and which tests and certifies organizations for compliance with those standards.

ISO 9001: An internationally recognized standard for quality management. Over 1 million organizations are currently certified, making this the most widely used standard in the world.

ISO 14001: An internationally recognized standard for environmental management.

ISO 22320: An internationally recognized standard for Emergency Management.

Job Action Sheet: A set of concise, step-by-step instructions, for use in the activation of any Key Role or subordinate job function, usually appended to the Emergency Response Plan. This provides an orientation to the work for the unfamiliar employee, and a memory aid for those assigned in advance to such functions. Such documents can be created for virtually any function in the emergency response. They are drawn from the concept of "standardized work" of Six Sigma and can also be used to both document the response and ensure compliance with policies and procedures.

Joint Commission: Formerly known as the Joint Commission on the Accreditation of Healthcare Organizations, it is a U.S.-based healthcare accreditation organization, which also operates internationally.

"Just-In-Time" Inventory Management: A Lean methodology in which the actual average consumption of a given resource within a given time-frame is calculated, and then in-house inventory levels are set to meet but not exceed those levels, with resupply occurring typically just prior to the exhaustion of stocks of the resource in question. In Lean, excess inventory is viewed as "waste" and this model is directed at eliminating inventory-related waste within an organization.

Lean for Healthcare: A management process for healthcare which has its origins in the manufacturing sector. The model concentrates on driving out all waste from the organization. It begins by identifying value-added and nonvalue-added steps to each part of the healthcare delivery process, focuses on the removal of nonvalue-added steps, where possible. Its application can result in positive impacts on productivity, quality, cost, and timely delivery of services.

Liaison Coordinator: The IMS Key Role responsible for the sharing and exchange of incident-related information with other agencies, but not with the media or the general public. This role is essential in gathering information upon which the Incident Manager will make some decisions and for the filtering of minutia from that information, so that the Incident Manager does not become overwhelmed. Part of the Command Group. This role is appointed by and reports to the Incident Manager.

Logic Tree: A logic-based process, central to the process of root cause analysis. This process is used to drive a process of investigation and inquiry which will ultimately lead to the underlying causes of a problem.

Logistics Chief: A member of the Key Role staff in IMS and a part of the control group. This role is responsible for analysis of resource requirements and the sourcing, acquisition, and delivery of the required resources. In a healthcare setting, this role often includes physical plant and support services such as security, housekeeping, dietary, and transportation. Supports the Operations Chief and the Incident Manager.

Magnitude: The likely impact that a hazard event will have, should it occur. Hazard events are normally ranked according to magnitude as a part of the HIRA process. In healthcare, magnitude may also be considered in terms of impacts on each of the five vulnerability variables.

Media Information Center: A controlled and secure point at which members of the media who are responding to an emergency may work, without any invasion of patient privacy or confidentiality or any disruption to the hospital's emergency operations. Here, the media can be provided with media releases and background material and may attend media conferences and conduct interviews.

Mitigation: Steps taken in advance of any disaster event, in order to either eliminate a potential hazard or to reduce its impact, should it occur. Such steps may be physical, procedural, or policy based.

Modified Mercalli Scale: A method of classifying and describing the severity of earthquake events, based upon the effects generated in the built environment.

MRI Scanner: Magnetic Resonance Imaging Scanner. A high-technology diagnostic imaging device which uses magnetic imaging to permit physicians to view various body systems selectively and in great detail. Capable of high-resolution imaging of soft tissue, unlike conventional X-rays.

National Fire Protection Association (NFPA): A trade association, operating primarily, but not exclusively in the United States, which creates and copyrights standards for firefighting, including firefighting equipment standards and model building codes for use by communities, and also standards for the management of emergency situations, including firefighting, hazardous materials response, rescue, and incident management. The organization has existed since 1896, and compliance with standards is voluntary.

Natural Hazard: A hazard event arising out of the weather, whether normal or severe, or out of the movement of earth (earthquakes, landslides, subsidence) or water (river and tidal flooding, storm surges, extreme storms, extreme heat and cold, etc.). Wildland fires are generally included in this category, although some of these are actually human caused.

Negative Pressure Ventilation: Mixed air supply with 100 percent exhaust outside of the building, ideally through a filtration system. Intended to prevent the movement of any airborne pathogen out of the room in which the patient is being cared for. Air flow is always from the corridor into the room, and *never* the reverse.

NIMS: A U.S.-based doctrine which promotes a comprehensive, systematic, nationwide approach to Emergency Management. It involves a common operating system and the interoperability of both communications and information management, along with standardized resource management.

Operational Period: A time span during the response to the emergency, used for planning, setting objectives, and service delivery purposes. This time span is set by the Incident Manager and normally corresponds to the business cycle of the command center, with a business cycle meeting occurring at the conclusion of each operational period, and before the start of the next.

Operations Chief: The IMS Key Role which is responsible for operating the "core" businesses of an organization, in this case, a healthcare facility. They are responsible for the provision of all care, including care of both victims and those patients already in the facility. In the event of evacuation, they are also responsible for the care and movement of all evacuees. The second most important role in IMS, after the Incident Manager. All other roles in the control group support this role.

Outbreak: The occurrence of one or more cases of a particular infection within a given community. The case numbers remain relatively small, and the disease has not migrated to other locations.

Pandemic: The global spread of an epidemic.

Pathogen: The specific microorganism which is responsible for any particular type of illness. These may be bacterial or viral in nature. Such organisms are often described by their mode of transmission (e.g., "airborne").

Planning Chief: The IMS Key Role which is responsible for the collection of information, research, analysis of findings, and short-term and long-term planning. This role is a part of the control group and supports both the Operations Chief and the Incident Manager.

Polygon: An irregularly shaped object, used on a map to define a given space. Such objects are often political, identifying electoral boundaries, such as wards, municipalities, counties, and states/provinces. Such objects can be used to plot data, such as risk exposure levels, spatially, for the purpose of comparison.

Preparedness: Those activities aimed at generating a level of ability to respond to any emergency event for which mitigation is not possible or practical. It can involve the creation of a HIRA, and the creation of an Emergency Response Plan and case-specific procedures. It can also involve the acquisition of required response resources, special training for staff, and exercises to test effective response.

Primary Patient/Case: The infectious patient/case from which all other patients/cases flow. Not necessarily the index patient/case.

Probability of Occurrence: The likelihood of a given disaster event occurring in a given location, based upon the number of times that such an event has occurred within the past 100 years. The information is simply a general guide and is research based. Usually expressed as a percentage of probability. To illustrate, if a given town has suffered from a documented ice storm 10 times in the past century, one can say that the probability of occurrence is 10 percent in any given year.

Product Identification Number (PIN): A system of standardized unique numbering, used by the chemical and transportation industries in order to reliably and correctly identify the contents of a package, container, vehicle, or rail car which is carrying hazardous materials, in case of any mishap during transit. The numbers are normally affixed to a placard on the outside of the package or vehicle. These can be used to provide rapid access to information regarding the identity of the substance, its properties, and basic safety procedures, in the event of an accidental release or other type of accident.

Project Management: A formal process for ensuring the successful completion of a given project. The project is usually broken down into individual steps along a timeline, and the order for those steps is identified, along with the ability of some steps to occur concurrently. The steps which are essential for the successful completion of the project (critical path) are identified. The work is assigned, progress is monitored, and any deviations from the project plan are corrected. Completion of the project is usually marked by a debrief, in order to identify unresolved issues and opportunities for improvement.

Project Plan: A diagram (usually a bar graph) used to identify all of the necessary steps for the completion of a project, the sequence of those steps and their relation to each other, and a timeline for the completion of both the individual steps and the project as a whole. The project plan permits the project leader to assign specific steps and to monitor for progress and completion and also the overall progress on project completion.

Public Information Coordinator: A member of the Command Group of the Incident Management Team, reporting directly to the Incident Manager. Tasked with dealing with all media inquiries and requests for information. Also tasked with the creation of media releases and background information sheets and also for operating the media information center, arranging media conferences, interviews, and tours, where appropriate.

QHA Trent: A British-based healthcare accreditation organization, operating not only throughout the United Kingdom, but also extensively in the European Union.

Quantitative Plotting: The creation of charts or graphs which display the occurrence of events, numbers of victims, quantities of individual items, or other resources, such as personnel. Such information may, in some cases, also be used spatially, to demonstrate distribution of any of the above factors.

Quarantine: Quarantine is a measure of isolation which is performed in order to prevent the spread of an infectious disease.

Radio Frequency Identification (RFID): A system in which the location and ongoing movement of resources and people may be tracked, using smaller, low-powered transmitter tags attached to objects, wristbands, or ID tags, which are tracked and reported by various sensors, distributed in a network around the building, most commonly installed in door frames. Such systems are becoming increasingly common in modern hospitals.

Ranking Model: A system of assigning a numeric value to events or their characteristics, and then arranging the events in numeric order, in order to set priorities for their management.

Rapid Intervention Team: A team of two to three medical personnel (usually a physician and one or two nurses) who function as a part of the facility's decontamination arrangements. These staff are specially trained, just as those performing the decontaminations. Their role is to remain outside of the decontamination "hot zone," partially suited in protective clothing, in order to be able to rapidly intervene, should an immediately life-threatening medical emergency occur during the decontamination process or should one of the staff performing the decontamination become injured and require removal.

Rate of Return: The frequency with which a given event recurs within a given set of locales. Some examples include "100-year floods" and "100-year storms."

Recovery: The phase of operation and activities which are directed at returning a community or an organization from a state of crisis to a state of normal or near-normal operating conditions. One of the four recognized stages of Emergency Management.

Response: The phase of operation and activities, following the occurrence of an emergency, which are directed at addressing the immediate effects of the emergency, ensuring public safety and care of the injured, protecting property and infrastructure, and the restoration of interrupted services.

Richter Scale: A method for the evaluation and description of the magnitude of earthquakes, based upon both seismograph readings and the effects upon the built environment. Although still popular with the media, this scale is gradually being replaced by the Modified Mercalli Scale in the scientific and Emergency Management fields.

Risk: Risk addresses potential impacts on human beings and their environment. It is largely driven by a combination of human presence, human activity, and the presence of built environment, relative to a given hazard. Risk is sometimes the result of conscious choice; however, risk can occur without a conscious choice, and a poor understanding or outright ignorance of a potential risk exposure.

Risk Acceptance: A decision, following the assessment and evaluation of a given risk, that mitigation or transference of the risk is either impossible or impractical and that operations will continue despite the presence of the risk exposure. This is the point at which preparedness activities such as the creation of an Emergency Plan and subordinate contingency plans usually begins.

Risk Aversion: A conscious decision to actively avoid an exposure to a risk. An example would be a Hospital Board examining a potential site for a new hospital beside a railway track, and, upon discovering that the railway moves hazardous goods trains on that track, making a decision to build the new hospital in another, less hazardous, location.

Risk Exposure: A specific set of circumstances in which a healthcare organization or a community subject to the effects of a given hazard.

Risk Management: A process for the specific management of risk exposures and determining how to deal with each type of risk exposure. Risks are identified, examined, analyzed, and communicated, and then decisions as to how to manage each are rendered. Options include acceptance, avoidance, mitigation, and transference.

Risk Mitigation: Those measures taken to reduce or eliminate problems, whether physical, policy driven, or process driven, which create specific exposures to risk events.

Risk Transference: Steps taken to move the vulnerability to a particular risk exposure from the facility to another location. This may involve the purchase of insurance protection or the outsourcing of a hazardous process or procedure to another location or organization.

Risk Treatment: The specific manner in which a given risk exposure is to be addressed within the organization (e.g., mitigation, transference).

Root Cause Analysis: A logic-based process, originating in the field of production engineering where it is often called "failure mode analysis," in which a specific process of research and logical examination is directed at establishing the actual underlying causes of vulnerability to a specific event.

Rotating Inventory Buffer: A system in which a small additional supply of a given resource is maintained in-house in a just-in-time inventory control model, in order to eliminate the "supply shock" generated by unforeseen events, such as mass casualty incidents in hospitals. New inventory is placed into the "buffer," with just-in-time deliveries occurring from the "buffer" to the point of use. By rotating the inventory, stale-dating and other forms of wastage are eliminated.

Safety Coordinator: A member of the IMS Command Staff, reporting to and supporting the Incident Manager. This role is tasked with the ongoing monitoring of safety related to all activities being conducted on-site and, in ideal circumstances, has the authority to order the immediate stoppage of any process or procedure that they believe to be unsafe. Also tasked with making recommendations to the Incident Manager for any changes to procedures or personal protective equipment which might make site operations safer.

Saffir–Simpson Scale: A method of describing and classifying hurricanes, according to wind speed, and of predicting the degree and type of damage to the built environment which is likely to be caused by a given storm.

Screening: An active process whereby all those entering a hospital facility in any capacity and for any reason are interviewed/inspected by trained staff and usually asked to complete a questionnaire regarding recent health status. They will also usually be asked to wash their hands with antibacterial cleanser. Based upon the outcome of the screening, they may be referred to a healthcare professional, such as a nurse, simply asked not to enter the facility, or permitted entry. The intent of this measure is to protect both those inside the facility and those visiting.

Scribe: An IMS support staff position, charged with the maintenance of all records related to the management of the emergency by the Incident Management Team, including the Event Log, resource/information requests, business cycle meeting minutes, and situation reports, on behalf of the Incident Manager. An essential role in a well-run command center.

Secondary Patient/Case: Those patients/cases which follow the primary patient/case in the chain of infection.

Secondary Treatment Area: A predesignated area within the facility where incoming patients who are assessed in triage with minor and some moderate injuries will be assessed and treated, in order to attempt to reserve the available space in the emergency department for high acuity patients, preventing the emergency department from becoming overwhelmed. A facility may incorporate multiple areas such as this into its Emergency Response Plan and focus individual areas on specific complaints or levels of acuity.

Situation Report (Sitrep): A formal report, outlining current status, progress made, and problems encountered, issued at regular intervals, usually following each business cycle meeting. This is a recognized method of sharing information with senior staff, outside agencies, other levels of government, and first responders.

Six Sigma: A system of process control and improvement which is intended to eliminate or greatly reduce potential errors in any type of manufacturing, service delivery, or other operating process. This system is in wide use in many types of private industry, and, increasingly, in public service sectors, as well.

Social Distancing: Avoiding large gatherings of individuals, in order to attempt to limit the transmission of infection within a community. This is probably the oldest known infection control measure.

Social Media: Electronic media used for the spreading of facts, thoughts, opinions, and images, both one to one, and to a broader, sometimes global, audience. Most such systems involve handheld devices, such as smartphones and computer tablets. Commonly used models at this writing include Facebook, Twitter, and Pinterest, among others, but new forms of this phenomenon appear almost every month. Some will succeed and grow massive in usership, while others will fade and die after only a few months.

Spatial Plotting: The display of variations of information and data across physical spaces, such as maps or floor plans. Such displays may consist of multiple point display or may employ either choropleths or polygons to identify variations in data.

Staging Area: A holding area in which resources are kept, prior to deployment and use. Hospitals typically have such locations for recalled staff to report to in a crisis. During hospital evacuation, staging areas are also employed to hold evacuated patients until they can be physically removed to other facilities.

Standardized Work: A Six Sigma-related process in which, as the name suggests, an absolutely consistent, zero-deviation process is designed and implemented for a specific procedure, in order to eliminate the occurrence of both deviation and potential errors.

Strike Team: An ICS/IMS term. A grouping of a single type of resource in order to accomplish a specific objective. As an example, a group of housekeeping staff assigned to the specific role of clearing, cleaning, and restaging the beds of discharged patients, in order to make them immediately available to the emergency department for admissions.

Supply Chain: The entire process by which a given resource travels from its manufacturer, through various stages and subprocesses, to the end user.

Supply Chain Management: A process by which supply chains are operated in order to improve speed and efficiency and to eliminate delays and waste.

Supply "Shock": A phenomenon which occurs during just-in-time inventory control, in which an unforeseen event, such as an MCI, may exceed the predicted normal usage of resources. The likely outcome is the rapid depletion of existing inventories, and the struggling of the system to be able to meet new levels of demand. In healthcare, this can sometimes result in the need to ration those limited resources which may be needed by large numbers of patients.

Support Staff: In IMS, those staff who do not occupy Key Roles such as Command or Control Staff but are nonetheless essential to the operation of the command center and the success of the Incident Management Team. Examples would include security, housekeeping, IT support, scribes, and so on.

Surge Capability: The potential for a hospital to use existing resources differently, in order to provide higher than normal levels of certain services during a disaster. An example would be the use of recovery room space as improvised intensive care space, thereby increasing the number of available ICU beds in the hospital over the short term.

Surge Capacity: The potential for a hospital to accept, triage, treat, and manage larger than normal numbers of patients during any type of emergency.

Suspect Patient/Case: Those individuals believed to be infected, and probably isolated, but for whom actual infection has not yet been clinically confirmed.

"Task Force": An IMS/ICS term. A multidisciplinary group tasked with a specific job. As an example, a Bed Clearance Task Force, moving from in-patient to in-patient on a ward, consisting of a physician who assesses the patient and writes the discharge orders, the charge nurse who manages the logistics of discharge, a discharge planner who makes arrangements for ongoing care and support, a representative from transportation who arranges the patient movement from the bed to the discharge lounge, and a representative from housekeeping who arranges the cleaning and preparation of the bed for the incoming patient.

Technological Hazard: A hazard which has been created by a production process or a transportation system.

Temporal Plotting: Plotting data variances graphically, using any type of time as the variable. Such plotting can reveal inconsistencies in risk exposure.

"Threshold of Disaster": The noted sociologist Niklas Luhmann described this as the point at which a disaster seems about to occur. He also described it as the point at which human risk perception finally becomes realistic, allowing unhindered preparedness and mitigation against disaster events.

Transmission: The movement of the disease pathogen from one patient to another. This can occur by various means, determined by the specific type of pathogen involved.

Treatment Area: A temporary area, usually improvised, within a hospital, for the emergency care and treatment of the ill and injured.

Triage: A process for the sorting and prioritization of incoming patients. Patients are usually categorized by clinical severity. Also occurs prior to arrival at hospital by EMS. May also occur to prioritize access to limited resources, such as cardiac monitors, ventilators, operating theaters, or intensive care beds.

Triage Area: A designated location in which triage occurs, prior to treatment.

Triage Categories: In a medical triage system, categories may include deceased, life threatening, serious, moderate, and minor injuries. The system may also identify whether or not the patient requires decontamination from hazardous materials exposure or whether this has already occurred.

UKICS: A variation of the incident command system, created by London's Metropolitan Police Service and now in common usage by all emergency services in the United Kingdom. The system differentiates the various levels of authority within each emergency service, using the terms "GOLD" (strategy level), "SILVER" (tactical level), and "BRONZE" (task level). Each emergency service will have its own designated people operating at each level but is permitted only one "GOLD" at any given time.

UPS: Uninterruptable power supply. A device or system used primarily in information technology, but also in some medical devices, which permits an uninterrupted flow of electrical power, and therefore continuous operation of the computer or device, during the period between a power failure and the initiation of emergency power or the resumption of normal power. Such devices are intended for transition only, and rarely operate continuously beyond two hours.

Value Stream Mapping: A Lean management principle which may be used to analyze the flow of any information or service delivery system, in order to identify delays, problems, and inherent weaknesses and to make such systems more effective, efficient, and resilient. Uses standardized symbols for each process, so a knowledge of the method is essential.

Vector: A means by which an infectious organism is physically carried from one physical location, such as a ward or even a hospital, to another. These may be patients, family members, unsuspecting staff members, or even ambulances.

VoIP: A technology which permits the use of the Internet, instead of conventional telephone systems, for the transmission of telephone calls. Also permits conversations from phone to computer, and computer to computer. Systems such as Skype and BlackBerry Messenger are examples of publicly available software of this type for general use. Many hospitals have converted to this less expensive technology as a cost-saving measure.

Vulnerability: The specific causes, whether physical, technical, or policy driven, why a community or a healthcare agency suffers adverse effects from a disaster event, should it occur. Often identified using root cause analysis.

Vulnerability Variables: The five areas of vulnerability normally considered in the assessment of a hospital or other healthcare provider, specifically: injury and loss of life, service disruption, physical plant damage, economic damage, and damage to reputation.

Zoonotic: An infectious disease outbreak which spreads from animals to humans.

Conclusion

The practice of Emergency Management in a healthcare setting is a complex process. All of the skills and challenges of "mainstream" Emergency Management are also present in this setting, but there are important differences. While the "mainstream" Emergency Manager must prepare for the protection of a potentially vulnerable community, his or her counterpart, operating in a healthcare setting, is responsible for protecting what is arguably the largest concentration of truly vulnerable people within that same community. In the community at large, crisis requiring the attention of the Emergency Manager is a relatively infrequent occurrence, whereas, in the healthcare setting, although the crises are generally on a smaller scale, such as a missing patient, a suspicious package, or an angry and distraught individual, crises may occur several times per day. After all, healthcare facilities do tend to be in the business of crisis management.

In the public setting, an Emergency Manager tends to be not so much a specialist, but a sophisticated generalist, functioning in an environment of elected officials and municipal or government department heads. Each of these is an expert of sorts in the operations and services of their own departments, but having limited experience in true crisis management. The mandate is to prepare a group of people who, apart from the three emergency services (police, fire, EMS), are probably not all that familiar with crisis management processes, to manage an infrequently occurring crisis of some sort.

Normal, day-to-day procedures and resource levels may require modification and a process of guidance from the operation of "business as usual" to "crisis response mode" and back again. The role of the Emergency Manager, in such settings, is not that of "specialist" so much as "sophisticated generalist," someone who has a working knowledge of the various municipal or government departments and whose job it is to create and manage a framework within which these individuals may cooperate and collaborate, even when they are unaccustomed to doing so on a daily basis, in order to manage and resolve whatever crisis has occurred.

In the healthcare setting, the Emergency Manager must not only be a sophisticated generalist, but also be a specialist of sorts, functioning in an intensely competitive environment of highly educated specialists, in which all procedures and services are driven by a combination of "best practice," research, and patient outcome. Every single patient to whom services are provided is either the victim of a current crisis or is recovering from the effects of an earlier crisis, and whether or not the people in such an environment have considered this before, the entire facility and its core business are all, in some fashion, about preparedness, response, recovery, and mitigation!

In any crisis response, the scope of practice for medical and care professionals within healthcare facilities remains the same; what differs is the scale of operation. Front-line staff already know about crisis response procedures, but require guidance and advance planning, in order to be able to, without prior warning, suddenly manage a surge in demand, in which a normal week's worth of seriously and critically ill or injured individuals arrives on the doorstep of the hospital in perhaps as little as two hours, and they must be able to do so safely, appropriately, and defensibly. In a society which is litigious, and this tendency is constantly increasing, the entire practice of Emergency Management within a healthcare facility has, arguably, as much to do with the ability to demonstrate "due diligence" after the fact, as it does with crisis response procedures.

Moreover, with technologies and services which are constantly changing and improving, the Emergency Manager must compete with highly educated and motivated department heads for limited funding on every project which is being considered or undertaken. In this environment, every funding and service proposal reaching the desk of the Chief Executive Officer has very likely been carefully crafted by an acknowledged "expert" in their respective field and has usually been impeccably researched to support its position in every single argument. In this environment, nothing less is considered acceptable.

There can be real challenges for the Emergency Manager when competing with a new patient care technology or an expanded scope of diagnostic or care services for the funding required for something which "might never happen," and the Emergency Manager working in a healthcare environment clearly requires an expanded skill set which "levels the playing field." What is required is a move to a practice of Emergency Management which is increasingly research based. The Emergency Manager must acquire and develop a working knowledge, and credentials, in both research skills and methodologies. In addition, the Emergency Manager in a healthcare setting can benefit tremendously from the acquisition of training in "mainstream" business techniques and skills. Any Emergency Manager, regardless of their location of practice, can benefit from this expanded skill set, but in the healthcare setting, it is absolutely essential for successful practice.

The "mainstream" business techniques which have proven useful in Emergency Management include, but are not limited to, several internationally recognized processes. The first of these is the process of Project Management. By utilizing internationally recognized processes, such as project plans, "Ishikawa" or "cause and effect" diagrams, Gantt charts, and a "critical path" approach, complex projects such as the HIRA, the Emergency Response Plan, the development of critical response procedures, and the creation and staging of emergency exercises become more efficient, effective, and manageable. These processes and associated techniques can even be applied to the operation of the business cycle of the healthcare facility's command center, with tremendous effect. For example, both Gantt charts and Ishikawa diagrams can be used to support the Incident Manager in the critical function of the monitoring of assignments for completion and actual progress throughout the business cycle, during the emergency itself.

The technique of "root cause" or "failure-mode" analysis, which can be used to analyze past problems and hopefully mitigate against their recurrence, also has a role to play in this setting. The use of such Project Management techniques as the Ishikawa diagram can also contribute to an effective analysis process. Such processes can be used during the business cycle to analyze problems which are occurring on an ongoing basis during any crisis. They are also highly effective, after the fact, in order to help determine what went wrong and why, so that procedures can be improved and mitigation measures put into place, so that the response to the next emergency is less problematic and more effective.

The techniques of the concepts of Six Sigma and Lean for Healthcare can also be used to great effect in preparing for any type of crisis response. The application of the principles of Lean for Healthcare can be used to create an Emergency Response Plan in which information and required instructions are far easier to both find and understand, making it much more likely that procedures and instructions in the plan will actually occur during the response to any emergency. The creation of pre-designed Job Action Sheets as "standardized work" checklists means that when a crisis does occur, the response will be predictable and correct, first time and every time, and that it will also be thoroughly and admissibly documented, within every branch of the organization. Together, these techniques can take the facility's Emergency Response Plan, in the minds of front-line staff, from a confusing document in which it is difficult to find anything, to a trusted resource and a "toolkit" containing almost everything that might be needed, to be relied on in any type of emergency.

Of equal importance is the fact that the use of such "mainstream" business techniques can also forge an important link between the Emergency Manager and the Senior Management Team of any healthcare facility. Most healthcare administrators are trained in business administration; they are not, or only rarely, clinicians themselves. Their jobs, like that of the Emergency Manager, are, in each individual case, to both create and operate the various aspects of the actual environment in which the clinicians work and provide their services. As such, almost all have had some level of prior exposure, including, in some cases, in-depth training, in the various "mainstream" business methods which have been proposed in this book as tools for the Emergency Manager. Information which has been prepared using these techniques will contain both familiarity and credibility for the target audience and will provide the input of the Emergency Manager with potentially far greater weight and influence in the management process.

The days of the Emergency Manager as a retired "cold warrior" have passed. Increasingly, instead of being trained on "short-courses" or drawn from the various emergency services, Emergency Managers are university-educated in their own specific discipline. Within healthcare, individuals used to become responsible for the Emergency Plan almost by accident, and in addition to a long list of "regular" duties! Today, the Emergency Manager is increasingly recognized and respected as a professional, and as a subject-matter "expert," in many of the fields in which they practice. The field will continue to grow and evolve, conducting research, reporting results, and, no doubt, developing its own new body of knowledge and techniques in its own right.

The practice of Emergency Management within any type of healthcare setting is certainly no exception to this evolution of the field. In fact, in the right circumstances, it has a potential to provide some level of leadership to the rest of the profession. While the use of the mainstream business tools and techniques described in this book for use in the healthcare setting is beginning to occur in some locales, they should become standard practices. While obtaining the training required in these techniques will require a good deal of effort by the individual Emergency Manager (it should become a part of basic education), it is clearly worth doing. In doing so, the practice of Emergency Management, wherever it occurs, can potentially become more efficient, more effective, and more credible. Emergency Managers, within the healthcare setting and beyond, can evolve into respected and essential contributors to the management processes of all types of institutions and environments.

Notes

Chapter 1

1. Elements of an Emergency Preparedness Plan (1999).
2. Shirley (2011).
3. Kerpchar and Protzman (2014), p. 61.
4. Shiver and Eitel (2009), p. 25.
5. Alexander (2002), p. 4.
6. Elements of an Emergency Preparedness Plan (1999).
7. Lean Six Sigma for Healthcare (2013).
8. Graban (2011), p. 50.
9. Introduction to Lean (2013).
10. Rottman, Shoaf, and Dorian (2005).
11. University of Toledo Medical Center Emergency Response Plan (2013).
12. Comprehensive Emergency Management Plan (1994).
13. Disaster Planning and Hospital Emergency Evacuation (2010).
14. Emergency Operations Plan (2013).
15. Hospital Emergency Operations Plan (2013).
16. Central State Hospital Emergency Operations Plan (2004).
17. A New Model for Healthcare (2014).
18. Duke University Hospital Fire/Life Safety Management Plan (2013).
19. Sorensen, Zane, Wante, Rao, Bortolin, and Rockenschaub (2011).
20. Emergency Codes in Hospitals and Health Care Facilities (2013).
21. Hospital Incident Command Job Action Sheets (2013).
22. University of Kentucky Hospital Emergency Management Plan (2013).

Chapter 2

1. Reilly and Markenson (2011).
2. Barr and Dowding (2015).
3. Prelas and Ghosh (2009).
4. Etter and Robinson (2010).
5. Veneema (2013).
6. Lowenthal (2002).
7. Adams, Gupta, and Wilson (2003).
8. Ammerman (1998).
9. Zidel (2006).
10. McGhee and McAliney (2007).

Chapter 3

1. Propper, Burgess, and Green (2002).
2. Joshi, Stahnisch, and Noseworthy (2009).
3. Risk and Compromise Tool (2012).
4. Bollin (2011).
5. Donahue and Tuohy (2006).
6. Viswanathan and Wizemann (2011).
7. FEMA (2004).
8. Bonnel and Smith (2010), p. 81.
9. Wrobel and Wrobel (2009), p. 45.
10. CNA (2009).
11. Ciottone and Biddinger (2015), p. 171.
12. Emergency Management and the Incident Command System (2013).
13. BlackBerry Emergency Response and Co-ordination (2013).
14. Eastaugh (1992), pp. 223–235.
15. Cantor, Hoogeveen, Robert, Elliott, Goldman, Sanderson, Plante, Prabhakar, and Miner (2012), pp. 201–206.
16. Supply Chain Metrics That Matter: A Focus on Hospitals (2013).
17. Reilly and Markenson (2010), pp. 226–231.
18. Provincial Hospital Resource System (PHRS)—Frequently Asked Questions (2012).
19. Region F Healthcare Preparedness Coalition (2013).

References

A New Model for Healthcare. 2014. Ontario Hospital Association Webpage. www.mediasite.oha.com/2014/Oct.02,2014_-_Emergency_Prep_-_IMS/ Handout.pdf (accessed February 07, 2016).

Adams, C., P. Gupta, and C. Wilson. 2003. *Six Sigma Deployment,* p. vii. New York, Routledge. ISBN: 978-0-7506-7523-9.

Alexander, D. 2002. *Principles of Emergency Planning and Management,* p. 4. Oxford, UK: Oxford University Press. ISBN: 978-1903544106.

Ammerman, M. 1998. *The Root Cause Analysis Handbook: A Simplified Approach to Identifying, Correcting and Reporting Workplace Errors,* p. 63. New York, NY: Productivity Press. ISBN: 9780527763268.

Barr, J. and L. Dowding. 2015. *Leadership in Health Care,* p. 20. London: Sage Publications. ISBN: 978-1473943339.

BlackBerry Emergency Response and Co-ordination. 2013. Covenco Disaster Recovery Services Webpage. www.covenco-dr.co.uk/disaster-recovery-services/ blackberry-emergency-response-and-coordination.htm (accessed February 04, 2014).

Bollin, S. 2011. *The Day After: Recovery Efforts at St. John's Mercy Joplin.* State of Iowa Health Department Webpage, PowerPoint presentation. www.iowadnr.gov/Portals/idnr/uploads/waste/P2%20Workshops%20 Resources/11oct05joplin.pdf (accessed February 04, 2014).

Bonnel, W. and K. Smith. 2010. *Teaching Technologies in Nursing and the Health Professions: Beyond Simulation and Online Courses,* p. 81. New York, NY: Springer Publishing. ISBN: 978-0826118486.

Cantor, W.J., P. Hoogeveen, A. Robert, K. Elliott, L.E. Goldman, E. Sanderson, S. Plante, M. Prabhakar, and S. Miner. 2012. "Prehospital Diagnosis and Triage of ST-Elevation Myocardial Infarction by Paramedics Without Advanced Care Training." *American Heart Journal, Am Heart J* 164, no. 2, pp. 201–206.

Central State Hospital Emergency Operations Plan. 2004. .pdf document. www .centralstatehospital.org/policy/Plan8.01090905.pdf (accessed January 31, 2014).

Ciottone, G.R. and P.D. Biddinger. 2015. *Ciottone's Disaster Medicine,* p. 171. New York, NY: Elsevier Health Sciences. ISBN: 978-0323358460.

CNA. 2009. *Medical Staff Credentialing: Eight Strategies for Safer Physician and Provider Privileging.* CNA, Chicago: Vantage Point magazine, 09:3. www .cna.com/vcm_content/CNA/internet/Static%20File%20for%20Download/ Risk%20Control/Medical%20Services/MedStaffCredentialing.pdf (accessed February 04, 2014).

Comprehensive Emergency Management Plan. 1994. State of Florida Regulation, .pdf document. www.fdhc.state.fl.us/MCHQ/Plans/pdfs/cemp.pdf (accessed January 31, 2014).

Disaster Planning and Hospital Emergency Evacuation. 2010. Adventist Risk Management Incorporated, .pdf document. www.adventistrisk.org/Portals/0/RMC/International%20Issues/HOSPITAL%20EMERGENCY%20EVACUATION%20--%20RMC%202011.pdf (accessed January 31, 2014).

Donahue, A.K. and R.V. Tuohy. July 2006. "Lessons We Don't Learn: A Study of the Lessons of Disasters, Why We Repeat Them, and How We Can Learn Them." *Journal of the Naval Postgraduate School Center for Homeland Defence and Security*, .pdf document. www.hsaj.org/?fullarticle=2.2.4 (accessed February 04, 2014).

Duke University Hospital Fire/Life Safety Management Plan. 2013. Duke University, .pdf document. www.opeiu391.org/browse/a2V5d29yZD1ob3 NwaXRhbCtlbWVyZ2VuY3krbWFuYWdlbWVudCtwbGFuK2 V4YW1wbGUmbGluaz1odHRwJTNBJTJGJTJGd3d3LnNhZm V0eS5kdWtlLmVkdSUyRkVvY19QbGFucyUyRkZpcmVVQcm V2ZW50aW9uTWFuYWdlbWVudFBsYW4ucGRm (accessed January 31, 2014).

Eastaugh, S.R. 1992. "Hospital Specialization and Cost-Efficiency: The Benefits of Trimming Product Lines." *Hosp Health Serv Adm* 37, no. 2, pp. 223–235, Summer. PMID: 10118589.

Elements of an Emergency Preparedness Plan. 1999. The Hartford Loss Control Department, .pdf document. www.accem.org/pdf/planelements.pdf (accessed January 31, 2014).

Emergency Codes in Hospitals and Health Care Facilities. 2013. Government of Western Australia, Department of Health Information Circular. www.health .wa.gov.au/CircularsNew/pdfs/12974.pdf (accessed February 07, 2016).

Emergency Management and the Incident Command System. 2013. US Department of Health and Human Services Webpage. www.phe.gov/Preparedness/planning/mscc/handbook/chapter1/Pages/emergency management.aspx (accessed February 04, 2014).

Emergency Operations Plan. 2013. Emergency Preparedness: Preparing Hospitals for Disasters. California Hospital Association Website. www.cal hospitalprepare.org/emergency-operations-plan (accessed January 31, 2014).

Etter, R. and P.A. Robinson. 2010. *Writing and Designing Manuals*, 3rd ed., p. 1. Boca Raton, FL: CRC Press. ISBN: 978-1420032918.

FEMA. 2004. *NIMS and the Incident Command System: A Position Paper*. Washington: US Federal Emergency Management Agency. www.fema.gov/txt/nims/nims_ics_position_paper.txt (accessed February 04, 2014).

Graban, M. 2011. *Lean Hospitals: Improving Quality, Patient Safety, and Employee Engagement,* 2nd Ed., p. 50. Boca Raton, FL: CRC Press. ISBN: 978-1439870440.

Hospital Emergency Operations Plan. 2013. New York, NY: University Hospital of Brooklyn, .pdf document. http://training.fema.gov/EMIWeb/edu/docs/nimsc2/NIMS%20-%20Lab%2010%20-%20Handout%20 10-13-Hospital%20EOP.pdf (accessed January 31, 2014).

Hospital Incident Command Job Action Sheets. 2013. University of Toledo, Environmental Health and Radiation Safety Webpage. www.utoledo .edu/depts/safety/Hospital_Incident_Command_Job_Action_Sheets.html (accessed January 31, 2014).

Introduction to Lean. 2013. Canadian Province of Saskatchewan, Health Department Webpage. www.health.gov.sk.ca/lean-introduction (accessed January 31, 2014).

Joshi, N.P., F.W. Stahnisch, and T.W. Noseworthy. 2009. *Reassessment of Health Technologies: Obsolescence and Waste.* Ottawa: Canadian Agency for Drugs and Technologies in Health, .pdf document. www.cadth.ca/media/pdf/494_Reassessment_of_HT_Obsolescence_and_Waste_tr_e.pdf (accessed February 04, 2014).

Kerpchar, J. and C. Protzman. 2014. *Leveraging Lean in the Emergency Department: Creating a Cost-Effective, Standardized, High-Quality, Patient-Focused Operation,* p. 61. Boca Raton, FL: CRC Press. ISBN: 978-1482237320.

Lean Six Sigma for Healthcare. 2013. American Society for Quality Webpage. http://asq.org/healthcaresixsigma/lean-six-sigma.html (accessed January 31, 2014).

Lowenthal, J.N. 2002. *Six SIGMA Project Management: A Pocket Guide,* p. 37. Milwaukee, WI: ASQ Quality Press. ISBN: 978-0873895194.

McGhee, P. and P. McAliney. 2007. *Painless Project Management: A Step-by-Step Guide for Planning, Executing, and Managing Projects,* p. 58. New York, NY: Wiley & Sons. ISBN: 978-0-470-17518-7.

Prelas, M.A. and T.K. Ghosh. 2009. *Science and Technology of Terrorism and Counterterrorism,* 2nd ed., p. 207. Boca Raton, FL: CRC Publications. ISBN: 978-1420071825.

Propper, C., S. Burgess, and K. Green. 2002. *Does Competition Between Hospitals Improve the Quality of Care? Hospital Death Rates and the NHS Internal Market.* University of Bristol Webpage. www.efm.bris.ac.uk/ecsb/papers/deaths.pdf (accessed February 04, 2014).

Provincial Hospital Resource System (PHRS)—Frequently Asked Questions. 2012. Gov't of Ontario (Canada) Criticall System Webpage. http://criticall.org/webconcepteurcontent63/000023720000/upload/pdf/PHRSFAQsApril202012.pdf (accessed February 04, 2014).

Region F Healthcare Preparedness Coalition. 2013. Georgia Department of Public Health, North Central Health District Webpage. http://northcentralhealthdistrict.org/emergency-preparedness/region-f-healthcare-preparedness-coalition/ (accessed February 04, 2014).

Reilly, M.J. and D. Markenson. October 2010. "Hospital Referral Patterns: How Emergency Medical Care is Accessed in a Disaster." *Disaster Med Public Health Prep* 4, no. 3, pp. 226–231. Doi: 10.1001/dmp.2010.30, PMID: 21149219.

Reilly, M.J. and D.S. Markenson. 2011. *Health Care Emergency Management: Principles and Practise*, p. 92. Sudbury Mass: Jones and Bartlett Learning. ISBN: 9780763755133 076375513.

Risk and Compromise Tool. 2012. On-Pace, Ohio State University Webpage. http://onpace.osu.edu/posts/documents/Risk%20and%20Compromise%20Tool.pdf (accessed February 04, 2014).

Rottman, S.J., K.I. Shoaf, and A. Dorian. 2005. Writing A Disaster Plan: A Guide For Health Departments, UCLA Centre for Public Health and Disasters, .pdf document. ftp://ftp.cdc.gov/pub/phlpprep/Legal%20Preparedness%20for%20Pandemic%20Flu/8.0%20-%20Non-Governmental%20Materials/8.6%20Writing%20a%20Disaster%20Plan%20-%20UCLA.pdf (accessed January 31, 2014).

Shirley, D. 2011. *Project Management for Healthcare*. Boca Raton, Fl: CRC Press. ISBN 9781439819531.

Shiver, J.M. and D. Eitel. (Eds.). 2009. *Optimizing Emergency Department Throughput: Operations Management Solutions for Health Care Decision Makers*, p. 25. Boca Raton, FL: CRC Press. ISBN: 978-1420084979.

Sorensen, B.S., R.D. Zane, B.E. Wante, M.B. Rao, M. Bortolin, and G. Rockenschaub. 2011. *Hospital Emergency Response Checklist: An All-Hazards Tool For Hospital Administrators And Emergency Managers*. World Health Organization, .pdf document. www.euro.who.int/__data/assets/pdf_file/0020/148214/e95978.pdf (accessed January 31, 2014).

Supply Chain Metrics That Matter: A Focus on Hospitals. 2013. Supply Chain Insights Webpage, Slide #7. http://supplychaininsights.com/supply-chain-metrics-that-matter-a-focus-on-hospitals/ (accessed February 04, 2014).

University of Kentucky Hospital Emergency Management Plan. 2013. US Federal Emergency Management Agency, .pdf document. http://training.fema.gov/EMIWeb/edu/docs/nimsc2/NIMS%20-%20Lab%2010%20-%20Handout%2010-14-U%20of%20KY%20Hosp%20EMP.pdf (accessed January 31, 2014).

University of Toledo Medical Center Emergency Response Plan. 2013. University of Toledo, .pdf document. www.utoledo.edu/depts/safety/docs/EP-08-009.pdf (accessed January 31, 2014).

Veneema, T.G. 2013. *Disaster Nursing and Emergency Preparedness for Chemical, Biological, and Radiological Terrorism and Other Hazards*, p. 58. New York, NY: Springer Pub. Co. ISBN: 9780826108647 0826108644.

Viswanathan, K. and T. Wizemann. 2011. *Preparedness and Response to a Rural Mass-Casualty Incident: Workshop Summary*, p.54. Washington, DC: National Academies Press. ISBN: 978-0309177177.

Wrobel, R.A. and S.M. Wrobel. 2009. *Disaster Recovery Planning for Communications and Critical Infrastructure*, p. 45. Boston, MA: Artech House. ISBN: 978-1596934696.

Zidel, T. 2006. *A Lean Guide to Transforming Healthcare: How to Implement Lean Principles in Hospitals, Medical Offices, Clinics, and Other Healthcare Organizations*, p. 28. Milwaukee: ASQ Quality Press. ISBN: 0873897013 9780873897013.

About the Author

Norm Ferrier has worked in various aspects of Canadian healthcare for more than 42 years, and for 32 of those years has focused increasingly on emergency planning for all types of healthcare facilities and organizations, across the entire continuum of healthcare. Norm holds a Master of Science degree in Emergency Planning and Disaster Management from the University of Hertfordshire, in the United Kingdom. He holds a Certificate in Healthcare Emergency Management from the Ontario Hospital Association and is a member of the Institute of Civil Protection and Emergency Management. Norm was the principal investigator for the Government of Canada's National Assessment of Emergency Planning in Canada's General Hospitals and was on the faculty of the Ontario Hospital Association, where he designed and taught courses related to Emergency Management for those who manage all aspects of healthcare, both across Canada and beyond.

Norm was also the Chair of the team which restandardized the Ontario Hospital Association's Standardized Emergency Colour Codes and coauthored the Ontario Hospital Association's Emergency Management Toolkit. He also created and introduced the Ontario Hospital Association's Certificate in Healthcare Emergency Management. Norm has been published and speaks internationally and is the author of another college/university textbook, *Fundamentals of Emergency Management: Preparedness*, published by Emond-Montgomery. Norm was the 2013 winner of the Canadian Emergency Management Award, presented at the World Conference on Disaster Management. He lives in Tavira, Portugal, where he still operates an Emergency Management consulting practice, focused primarily, but not exclusively, on healthcare.

Index

OTHER TITLES IN THE HEALTHCARE MANAGEMENT COLLECTION

- *Better Outcomes* by Rafael E. Salazar
- *Emergency Management for Healthcare, Volume IV* by Norman Ferrier
- *Emergency Management for Healthcare, Volume III* by Norman Ferrier
- *Emergency Management for Healthcare, Volume II* by Norman Ferrier
- *Emergency Management for Healthcare, Volume I* by Norman Ferrier
- *Strategic Data Management for Successful Healthcare Outcomes* by Lakkaraju Hema
- *Improv to Improve Healthcare* by Candy Campbell
- *Integrated Delivery* by David Stehlik
- *Mastering Evaluation and Management Services in Healthcare* by Stacy Swartz
- *Lean Thinking for Emerging Healthcare Leaders* by Arnout Orelio
- *Process-Oriented Healthcare Management Systems* by Anita Edvinsson
- *Behind the Scenes of Health Care* by Hesston L. Johnson
- *Predictive Medicine* by Emmanuel Fombu

Concise and Applied Business Books

The Collection listed above is one of 30 business subject collections that Business Expert Press has grown to make BEP a premiere publisher of print and digital books. Our concise and applied books are for…

- Professionals and Practitioners
- Faculty who adopt our books for courses
- Librarians who know that BEP's Digital Libraries are a unique way to offer students ebooks to download, not restricted with any digital rights management
- Executive Training Course Leaders
- Business Seminar Organizers

Business Expert Press books are for anyone who needs to dig deeper on business ideas, goals, and solutions to everyday problems. Whether one print book, one ebook, or buying a digital library of 110 ebooks, we remain the affordable and smart way to be business smart. For more information, please visit www.businessexpertpress.com, or contact sales@businessexpertpress.com.